122 YEARS ON THE OLD BAY LINE

JACK SHAUM

FEATURING THE PHOTOGRAPHY OF HANS MARX

AMERICA THROUGH TIME®
ADDING COLOR TO AMERICAN HISTORY

In memory of Captain Samuel B. Chapman and Captain Patrick L. Parker

"There never was a method of domestic transportation so pleasant as the night boat. Further, I doubt that any transportation medium was ever as satisfying esthetically as the big night boat."

George W. Hilton, author of The Night Boat

America Through Time is an imprint of Fonthill Media LLC
www.through-time.com
office@through-time.com

Published by Arcadia Publishing by arrangement with Fonthill Media LLC
For all general information, please contact Arcadia Publishing:
Telephone: 843-853-2070
Fax: 843-853-0044
E-mail: sales@arcadiapublishing.com
For customer service and orders:
Toll-Free 1-888-313-2665

www.arcadiapublishing.com

First published 2022

ISBN 978-1-63499-399-9

Typeset in 10pt on 13pt Sabon
Printed and bound in England

Foreword

Why write a book on the Old Bay Line? It has been almost sixty years since it stopped operating and its steamers have long since disappeared. Now, in this third decade of the twenty-first century, steamboats in general are fading from the public consciousness and are in danger of possibly being forgotten. Today's methods of travel have little in common with the pleasantries of sailing on Chesapeake Bay aboard a steamboat, but steamboats should not be forgotten as they played an important role in the development of transportation and the economy in this country. In their later years, they took passengers back into history so they could experience travel the way their forebears did. All one had to do was step aboard. That is what I did at the age of eight, and that first twelve-hour voyage down the bay was as exciting to me as a transatlantic crossing and sparked a lifetime passion for steamboats.

A voyage on the Old Bay Line meant different things to different people. For much of its long history until the establishment of the automobile, travelers needing fast, reliable, and comfortable transportation to Norfolk or Baltimore, or to make reliable rail connections at either port, turned to the steamers. Businessmen with meetings in either Baltimore or Norfolk could count on the boats for a respite from the daily office routine while getting a restful night's sleep so that they arrived at their destination fully refreshed for a day's work.

By the mid-twentieth century, when the boats were no longer the quickest method of transportation, they attracted a new clientele—vacationers seeking pleasure trips on Chesapeake Bay that were steeped in history. Many of the children traveling with their families saw the trip as a real adventure, and if they were lucky—as I was—the captain took them under his wing and perhaps allowed them to take the wheel for a few minutes or blow the whistle. Soldiers and sailors attached to the government installations around Hampton Roads traveled on the night boats to get to and from new military assignments or for a trip home on liberty. Also, in the last decades, when the steamers were the only ones of their kind remaining in service anywhere in the country, there were maritime enthusiasts and historians for whom a trip on a vintage steamer was tantamount to a pilgrimage. Yet no matter what a person's reason was for taking the Old Bay Line, they were assured of good accommodation and the finest courteous, reliable service.

This colorful letterhead was used by the Old Bay Line for many decades.

A voyage to Norfolk on the Old Bay Line in the 1950s and 1960s began at Pier Three, Pratt Street, on Baltimore's inner harbor. (*Photo by Hans Marx*)

Arriving at the Old Bay Line pier, passengers were greeted by white-jacketed stewards who saw to it that their luggage was delivered to the proper stateroom. They were led up to the second level of the pier where they crossed the gangway onto the vessel's forward deck to be greeted by a ship's officer. Stepping inside immediately transported the travelers back to another era. The long corridors stretched nearly the entire length of the steamer and were finished in "Old Ivory" with touches of mahogany here and there and were illuminated by numerous lights in fancy brass receptacles. The decks were carpeted in most areas, except certain large bedrooms that had hardwood floors. Overhead, there was a large stained-glass skylight with intricate ceiling carvings surrounding it. Light also entered overhead through leaded clerestory windows. Stairways leading to the main deck below (also called the freight deck) were surrounded by mahogany and wrought-iron balustrades.

Before going to their staterooms, the passengers stopped at the purser's office on the saloon deck (second deck above the waterline) to pick up their big brass stateroom keys. As late as 1961, per-person passenger fares were as low as $5.80 one way, $10 for a round-trip, with stateroom charges ranging from $2 to $6.25 per room. Multiple doors lining the corridors led to the staterooms, most of which were outside rooms with windows. There were several different types of accommodations. They included basic upper and lower berth rooms with a basin, chair, reading lamp, and fan; bedrooms with toilet and showers; bedrooms with double and twin beds with toilet, shower, and tub; and family bedrooms with all facilities that connected with one another to create a small suite. All rooms had individual heat controls and hot and cold running water. Every room also had a rack on the bulkhead holding a pitcher of water and drinking glasses—a tradition going back to the earliest days of steamboats on the bay.

Every stateroom had a posted notice with information for passengers to help them get acclimated. One item on the notice stands out, warning passengers about playing cards with strangers—a holdover from the nineteenth century when card sharks could be found regularly on steamboats everywhere. A separate framed notice contained safety information, including instructions for putting on a life jacket and telling what lifeboat station the occupants of that room were assigned to.

Two grand staircases with ornamental wrought-iron work and mahogany railings linked the saloon and gallery (third deck above the water) decks, one in the forward part of the vessel and one in the aft section. The fronts of the steps were finished in gleaming brass facing and both staircases were surmounted by large mirrors. Beneath the mirror was the ship's ornate carved wooden builder's plate.

Public rooms included the dining room, located forward on the gallery deck; the social hall; smoking room; and a music room with a piano where informal musicales among passengers could take place. The public spaces also included the two-deck indoor lounge areas surrounded by galleries of decorative wrought iron.

"All ashore that's going ashore" was announced over the public address system fifteen minutes before the scheduled 6:30 departure. The last of the freight was secured, and the big freight gangway ports were closed and secured for the twelve-hour run down the bay. Then precisely on time as advertised, the mooring lines were brought in, and passengers felt a low rumble below them as the engine came to life and the steamer began backing into the harbor. Her melodious steam whistle gave out three blasts, announcing that she was underway and going astern. Passengers lined the rails as the vessel swung around in the harbor basin until she was facing down the Patapsco River toward the open bay.

Above left: Once aboard, passengers entered into the forward lounge on the saloon deck where, surrounded by Edwardian elegance, they stopped at the purser's office to pick up their big, brass stateroom keys. (*Photo by Edward O. Clark*)

Above right: Overhead was a dome of intricate stained glass surrounded by ornate carvings and a clerestory of leaded glass. (*Photo by Hans Marx*)

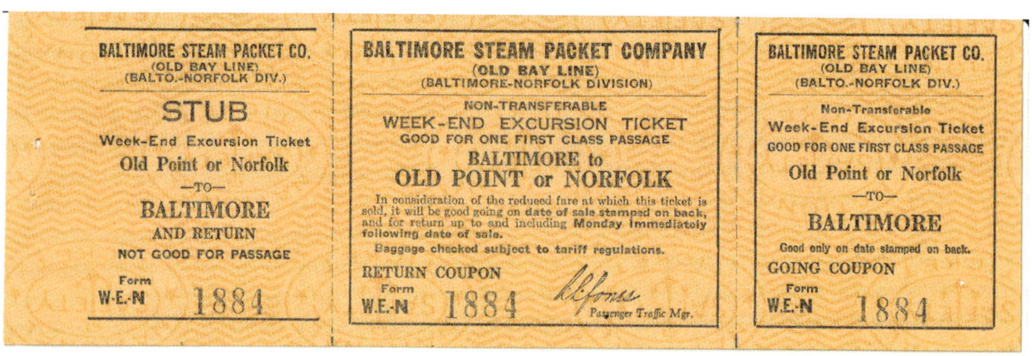

BALTIMORE STEAM PACKET CO.
(OLD BAY LINE)
(BALTO.-NORFOLK DIV.)
STUB
Week-End Excursion Ticket
Old Point or Norfolk
—TO—
BALTIMORE
AND RETURN
NOT GOOD FOR PASSAGE
Form W-E-N 1884

BALTIMORE STEAM PACKET COMPANY
(OLD BAY LINE)
(BALTIMORE-NORFOLK DIVISION)
NON-TRANSFERABLE
WEEK-END EXCURSION TICKET
GOOD FOR ONE FIRST CLASS PASSAGE
BALTIMORE to
OLD POINT or NORFOLK
In consideration of the reduced fare at which this ticket is sold, it will be good going on date of sale stamped on back, and for return up to and including Monday immediately following date of sale.
Baggage checked subject to tariff regulations.
RETURN COUPON
Form W.E-N 1884
Passenger Traffic Mgr.

BALTIMORE STEAM PACKET CO.
(OLD BAY LINE)
(BALTO.-NORFOLK DIV.)
Non-Transferable
Week-End Excursion Ticket
GOOD FOR ONE FIRST CLASS PASSAGE
Old Point or Norfolk
—TO—
BALTIMORE
Good only on date stamped on back.
GOING COUPON
Form W.E-N 1884

Each passenger was issued a ticket like this that covered transportation only on the steamer. There was a separate stateroom charge.

BALTIMORE STEAM PACKET CO.

(OLD BAY LINE)

INFORMATION

Tickets will be collected at passenger gangway in morning when leaving steamer. Passengers not having tickets will please purchase same at the Purser's office.

Lock doors and shutters when leaving room and before retiring.

A safe where money and valuables may be checked is in the Purser's office.

The Company is not responsible for articles left on steamer, search room and berth before vacating.

Trunks are not allowed in staterooms or cabins.

Dogs and other pets are not allowed in staterooms, cabins or salons.

You are warned against playing cards with strangers.

Smoking is not allowed in staterooms.

Passengers for Old Point are requested to notify the Purser's office so they may be called in time.

Please leave stateroom key in door when leaving the steamer.

Medicine chest with first aid and emergency remedies is kept aboard steamer. Apply to Purser.

Ladders to assist passengers to upper berths may be obtained from the Bell-boy.

Taxicabs meet steamer for transfer of passengers holding through tickets to the different railroad stations in Baltimore. Last taxicab leaves at 8 a. m.

DINING ROOM LOCATED ON GALLERY DECK FORWARD

BREAKFAST

Club and a la carte bginning at 6:00 a. m.

DINNER

Table d'hote from 6:30 to 8:30 p. m. A la carte until 9:30 p. m.

THE PRICE OF THIS ROOM IS $4.50

A framed notice like this was mounted on the bulkhead in each stateroom. There was a similar framed notice covering safety issues.

Above left: Departure time—promptly at 6:30 p.m., the steamer sounded three blasts on her whistle announcing that she was backing from her pier. (*Photo by the author*)

Above right: The *City of Norfolk* has backed out of her berth and is turning to head down the Patapsco River toward the Chesapeake Bay. (*Photo by Hans Marx*)

There were many sights as the vessel steamed through the busy port of Baltimore. Some of these students on board for a spring trip are looking at Fort McHenry (out of photo at right) and at a passing tanker on the other side. (*Photo by Hans Marx*)

There were lots of harbor activities for the travelers to take in—small tugboats scurrying around, ocean-going freighters and tankers alongside piers or at anchor awaiting berths, and an occasional excursion steamer returning from a trip to the bay resorts of Tolchester and Betterton. Coming into view shortly off to starboard as the steamer skirted Locust Point was the green expanse of Fort McHenry, where American forces turned back a British invasion in 1814, leading to the writing of "The Star-Spangled Banner."

Now, the passengers were faced with a choice—remain on deck awhile longer to take in the sights of the busy port, or head for the first sitting of dinner in the dining room. Quite often, the call to the dining room won out; the cuisine of the Old Bay Line was justly famous.

The dining room on the company's last two steamers—the *City of Richmond* and *City of Norfolk*—was located all the way forward on the gallery deck and had large windows giving an unobstructed view of passing landmarks and other vessels. Tables were covered in immaculate white linen and were set with heavy silverware and crockery—all bearing the insignia of the Old Bay Line. Bottled water was also on each table. In these surroundings, many passengers spent the first hour or so of their voyage.

In the warm weather months, there was still plenty of daylight after an early dinner, so many passengers strolled the outer decks to take in the sights and sounds of the Chesapeake Bay; the 4-mile-long Chesapeake Bay Bridge, then the longest all-steel over-water bridge in the world; the workboats of Bay watermen passing close at hand, taking their catch to market; and buoys marking the channel that blinked after dark, some sounding bells as they rocked in the waves. As darkness descended, lights came on along the shore on both sides of the bay, looking much like the stars filling the sky overhead. The steamer's deck lights cast a subdued glow, and in the darkened wheelhouse, the officers maintained a close watch.

At this point in the voyage, there were several different diversions available—after-dinner drinks or curling up with a good book in the lounge, informal music in the music room, and in the 1950s and 1960s, television was also available in the smoking room. Soon, however, passengers began drifting off to their staterooms to prepare for bed, and the lights in the public rooms were dimmed—a practice begun in the 1800s to encourage passengers to turn in. For those disembarking at Old Point Comfort at the entrance to Hampton Roads, the wakeup call would come very early as the steamer was due there at 5:30 a.m. Once between the crisp white sheets, the travelers were lulled to sleep by the gentle creaking of the woodwork and the soothing sound of the ship's wake, heard through the window shutters. It did not take long to fall asleep as the steamer continued on her way. Very few passengers, if any, were awake around 1 a.m. as the southbound steamer passed her northbound running mate near the mouth of the Potomac River.

"Old Point Comfort wharf at 5:30," intoned the steward as he knocked on the doors of passengers disembarking at the octagonal wharf at the U.S. Army's Fort Monroe with the imposing Hotel Chamberlin nearby. The landing at Old Point was popular with people wanting to visit the nearby historic sites at Jamestown, Williamsburg, and Yorktown. In the nineteenth century, it had several luxury hotels and was a favorite destination for vacationers seeking the sea air and mild climate, and the Old Bay Line had been calling there from its earliest years. There was also a significant amount of freight traffic at Old Point. The steamer quietly edged alongside the wharf, the lines were secured, the gangways were run out, and passengers and freight came off the boat. The visit at Old Point was brief and it was not long before the steamer had cast off and headed across Hampton Roads to Norfolk, just visible in the distance.

A bright orange rising sun filled the area with light as a fleet of workboats passed close by, headed out for a day's work harvesting the crabs, oysters, and fish for which the Chesapeake Bay is famous. Soon, the mammoth Norfolk Naval Base came into view off to port. The largest naval base in the world, it is home to the U.S. Atlantic Fleet, and it was not uncommon to see enormous aircraft carriers, battleships, destroyers, cruisers, and submarines at their docks as the steamer passed by. Then, as the naval base receded in the distance behind the vessel, she steamed past bustling commercial docks where ships loaded general freight and specialty cargoes such as coal at the imposing terminals off to port.

Finally, the steamer slowed and right on schedule, she nosed into the Old Bay Line wharf at the foot of Main Street, in Norfolk's busy downtown area. Once the ship was secured to the dock, it was back to the dining room, this time for a hearty Southern breakfast as freight was off-loaded below. Cheerful white-coated waiters made their way from table to table, taking meal orders and refilling coffee cups.

All too soon, the clocks neared 8:30 a.m. and it was time to go ashore. Once their tickets had been collected by a member of the purser's staff, the passengers crossed the gangway back onto land, and their pleasant voyage came to an end.

That is why this book was written—to keep alive the wonderful experience of traveling on an overnight steamboat in the hope that it will rekindle memories for past travelers and open a new area of interest for present generations who never knew the Old Bay Line.

Above: This sign was located over the doorway on the *City of Richmond* leading to the gangway and onto the pier.

Left: The author and his stepfather Harry Hafele aboard the *City of Richmond* for his first voyage in June 1954.

Acknowledgments

To say that this book had a long gestation period would be an enormous understatement, since I started collecting information on the Old Bay Line when I made my first voyage at the age of eight. Over the decades, I have been fortunate to have had a number of friends, many now departed, who shared my interest in the Old Bay Line and who contributed to it by giving me memorabilia and illustrations from their collections. It is impossible, given the passage of time, to recall everyone who contributed to my collecting, but there are those whose contributions stand out.

Anyone writing about the Old Bay Line owes a huge debt of gratitude to the late Alexander Crosby Brown, author of *The Old Bay Line, 1840–1940*, published on the occasion of the line's centennial, and followed up in 1961 with an updated version entitled *Steam Packets on the Chesapeake*. Both books continue to be an inspiration to me plus I was fortunate to have had Alec as a friend and mentor. Another valued friend was the late David C. Holly, author of four books on Chesapeake Bay steamboating that are models of what books of that type should be. The late H. Graham Wood probably knew more about Chesapeake Bay steamboats than any other single individual and was only too willing to share his knowledge with a young enthusiast. The late A. Spencer Marsellis shared his encyclopedic knowledge, illustrations, and ephemera. I am particularly happy to be able to feature several fine paintings by the late C. Leslie Oursler, two of which I am privileged to own. John W. S. Foster provided an illustration of his ancestor, steamboat executive Reuben Foster.

In more recent times, archivists at several institutions have assisted me in procuring rare illustrations. They include Eben Dennis and Debra Elfenbein at the Enoch Pratt Free Library's Special Collections unit, Lisa Williams at the Digital Services Department at the Mariners Museum, Jenifer Dolde and Katelyn Kean at the Chesapeake Bay Maritime Museum, Rob Hurry at the Calvert Marine Museum, Leslie Eames at the Maryland Center for History and Culture, Angela Schad at the Hagley Museum, and Anat Banin at the Central Zionist Archives.

I am particularly indebted to Marlene Malcan, executor of the estate of photographer Hans Marx, and her husband Jay, whose assistance cannot be overstated. They have been very supportive of the book project and opened up their vast archive of Mr.

Marx's outstanding collection to me. He had a great love for the Old Bay Line and did a tremendous job documenting its history over the course of several decades. I am proud to be able to feature his photographs in this book. I wish I could have known him.

At *America Through Time*, I have benefitted greatly from the guidance of Alan Sutton and Kena Longabaugh and their team of experts.

My wife Martha has always encouraged me in my research and writing work and for that support I am grateful beyond measure.

It has not always been easy keeping track of all the help I have received in so many ways over the course of so many decades of delving into the story of the Old Bay Line and to anyone I have overlooked, my sincere apologies.

All images not otherwise indicated are from the author's collection.

Contents

Foreword 3
Acknowledgments 11
Introduction 15

1 Early Steamboat Operations Between Baltimore and Norfolk 17
2 Fleet Expansion and Civil War 25
3 The "Old Established" Bay Line 31
4 Intense Competition 39
5 The Ultimate Bay Liners 55
6 Depression Years, Prohibition, and Tragedy 65
7 Cuisine on the Bay 76
8 On the Freight Deck 83
9 "When We Left, It Was Just a Fresh Breeze" 91
10 An Anniversary and a Merger 94
11 Called Up for War Service 100
12 Picking Up the Pieces After the War 112
13 What Might Have Been 121
14 Shadows Lengthen 128
15 The Last Night Boat 138

Epilogue 145
Endnotes 150
Bibliography 154
Index 157
About the Author 160

Introduction

It all began so simply.

A dispatch from *The* [Baltimore] *Sun's* legislative correspondent in the state capital in Annapolis on March 18, 1840, consisted of a single paragraph. There, between an item about a divorce proceeding before the Maryland General Assembly and another on a non-imprisonment for debt bill, was a single line that set the stage for a momentous chapter in the history of steam navigation on Chesapeake Bay: "A bill incorporating the Baltimore Steam Packet Company."[1] That was it. No fanfare and no speeches—just one line announcing the birth of a company that would become a maritime institution, and which would survive to become the oldest steamboat company in the United States, carrying passengers and freight on a nightly basis between Baltimore and Norfolk.

While it is true that there had been steamboats operating on Chesapeake Bay since 1813, most of those were independent operations that in many cases had only one vessel, flourished for a few years, and then quietly disappeared. The Baltimore Steam Packet Company, on the other hand, prospered to field fleets of steamers—fifty-three vessels in all over the company's long history—that became the standard against which many others on the bay were measured, ultimately achieving legendary status. It carried on for 122 years—a laudable record for any business enterprise.

Operating steamboats on the Chesapeake Bay in the early decades of the nineteenth century was not easy. The boats were small with many barely offering the most basic accommodations. There were times when their engines malfunctioned and the steamers had to finish their voyages under sail or be towed to port. There was the danger of explosions and fires. Nevertheless, those early pioneers persevered because they had faith in the steamboat—whether it was between Baltimore and Norfolk, Washington and Norfolk, up the bay toward Philadelphia, or across the Bay's wide waters and up the many rivers that make up Tidewater Maryland and Virginia.

It was a colorful, exciting, and fascinating era and we are the poorer because it has passed into history and can never be resurrected.

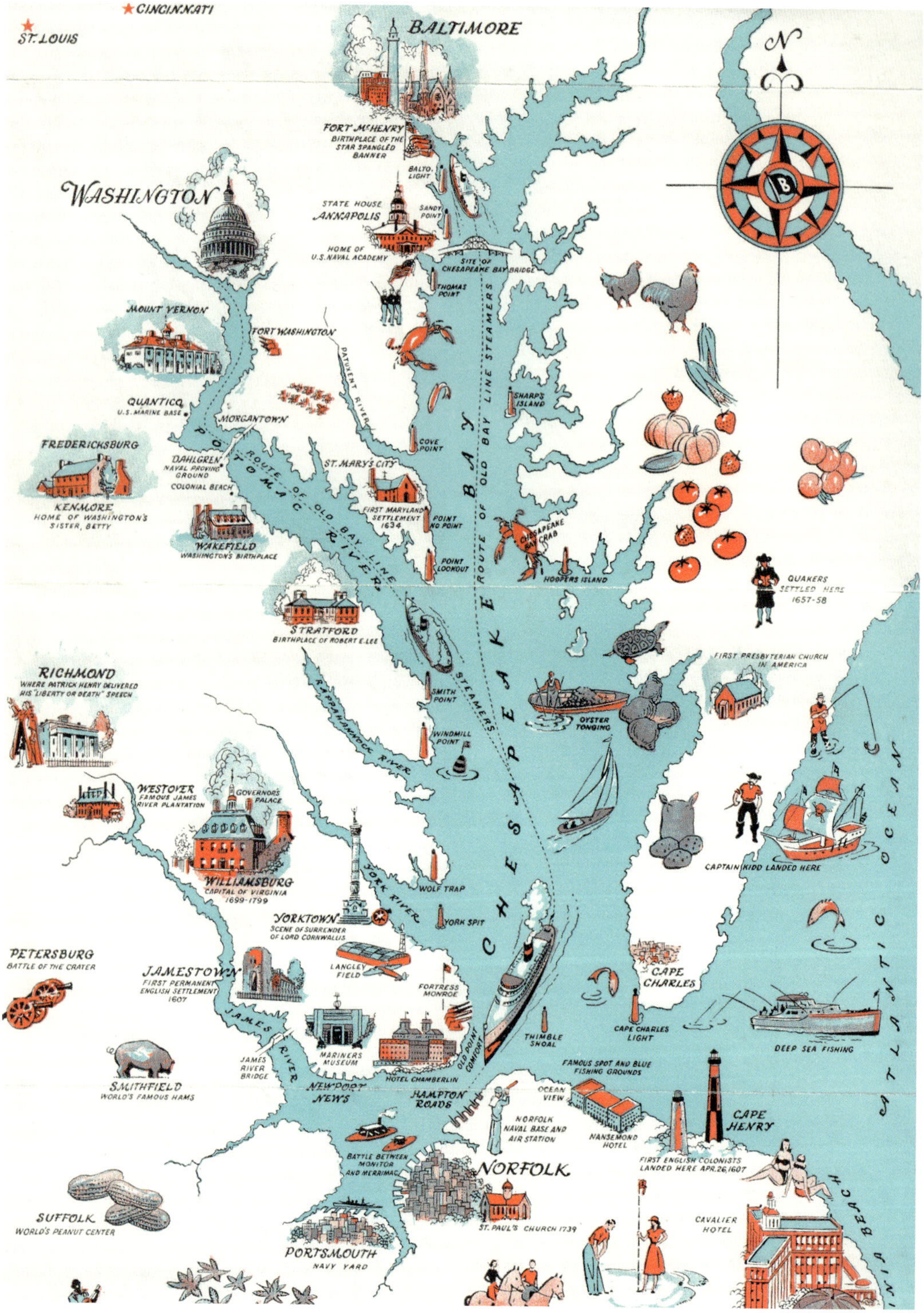

The routes traveled by the Old Bay Line between Baltimore and Norfolk and Washington and Norfolk.

1

Early Steamboat Operations Between Baltimore and Norfolk

The steamboat era on Chesapeake Bay lasted 148 years and ten months.

The first steamer on the bay, the *Chesapeake* with Captain Edward Trippe commanding, departed on her first voyage from Baltimore at 8 a.m. on Sunday, June 13, 1813. It was a round trip to Annapolis that returned later the same day. On Saturday, April 14, 1962, at 6:30 a.m., the *City of Norfolk* with Captain Patrick L. Parker commanding, completed her last overnight voyage from Norfolk carrying freight only and tied up for good.

Of those nearly 149 years, the Baltimore Steam Packet Company, better known as the Old Bay Line, was on the scene for 122 years, more than three-quarters of the entire steamboat era. When the company made its final runs in 1962, it had long outlasted all of its competitors on the bay and elsewhere.

The Old Bay Line epitomized what was best about the steamboat era on the Chesapeake—sturdy, reliable, and fast ships with handsome, comfortable overnight accommodations, outstanding cuisine, and sufficient space below decks for several hundred tons of freight. Its vessels operated year-round in all kinds of weather between Baltimore and Norfolk with a stop at Old Point Comfort, Virginia, on a schedule that rivaled the best passenger trains for on time performance.

The steamboat arrived on the scene at a time when travel by water in the Chesapeake region was not easy. If one wanted to cross the bay or travel its length, it was aboard a sailing ship. Early advertisements for sailing vessels often featured a departure time but rarely included an arrival time. Since the ship relied on the wind, the arrival time was often uncertain. Overland travel up and around the head of the bay was difficult because many of the roads were that in name only, and the stagecoaches that transported people had to contend with rough, dusty roads, icy roads, or ones mired in mud. A person wishing to travel between the eastern and western shores of the bay did so either by taking a bumpy stagecoach ride up and around the top of the bay, or a sailing ship whose arrival time was uncertain. Steamboats proved to be considerably more comfortable and reliable than the stagecoach and the sailing vessel. They opened a new era of transportation on Chesapeake Bay that was a major player in the economic development of the region.

The pacesetting steamer *Chesapeake* did not operate on the Baltimore–Norfolk run but was employed most often on the Union Line's route between Baltimore and Frenchtown

Captain Edward Trippe played an important role in the early development of the steamboat on Chesapeake Bay. (*Courtesy of The Mariners' Museum and Park, #P0001.016-01-(1590)*)

at the head of the bay. Her passengers transferred there to a stagecoach for a ride across the peninsula between Chesapeake Bay and Delaware Bay, then caught another steamer to complete their trip to Philadelphia or other northern points. Two men of note were instrumental in her operation—Captain Edward Trippe, her first master, who is considered by many to be the father of the steamboat on the bay, and Andrew F. Henderson, who would later become the first president of the Baltimore Steam Packet Company.

The first steamer to make a trip between Norfolk and Baltimore was the *Eagle*, which arrived in Baltimore from Philadelphia by way of Norfolk on June 25, 1815. The voyage up the bay from Norfolk had taken twenty-nine hours. On arrival in Baltimore, she was described as elegant and commodious. But she was not intended for the Baltimore–Norfolk run; she was on what today is called a positioning voyage to get her to her regular place of operation, which was on a line running between Baltimore and Elkton, also at the head of the bay. Her master on that voyage was Captain Moses Rogers, who made the first ever voyage in a steamboat on the open sea and who later commanded the steamship *Savannah* in 1819 when she became the first vessel to cross the Atlantic partially under steam power.

Many steamboats in those days were owned by individuals rather than a company. Those owners often wore several hats—that of purser, agent, and even captain, in addition to that of owner. They sold tickets and supervised the loading of the steamers among other things, in addition to overseeing the actual day-to-day operation of the boats. Newspaper advertisements for the early steamers often included the name of a single individual, who was listed as proprietor.

One of those individual proprietors was Benjamin Ferguson, who, in 1817, built the *Virginia*, the first steamer designed specifically for a regularly-scheduled Baltimore–Norfolk run. She was a wooden-hull sidewheeler 136 feet long with a beam of 24 feet and could do about 8 miles an hour, making the one-way voyage in about twenty-four hours. Like most other steamers of the period, she likely carried auxiliary sails in case of engine problems or if the supply of wooden logs burned for fuel ran out before the boat reached port.

The two cities are about 185 miles apart and were well suited for regular steamboat service. The *Virginia* arrived in Norfolk from Baltimore on a shakedown trip for the first time on July 31, 1817, and according to a news report, her passengers stated that "The Table could not be better furnished—bedding surpassing any they had seen—and in short, every thing [*sic.*] that could render the journey smooth and pleasant." Her regular service between the two cities began on August 22 and she also made occasional excursions to places like Jamestown, Virginia, and Annapolis, Maryland, between regular runs.[1]

There were other steamers besides the *Virginia* that sometimes sailed on the Baltimore–Norfolk route, including the *Richmond*, *Petersburg*, *Surprise*, and *Roanoke*, among others. The steamer *Norfolk*, which had operated on the James River and in North Carolina, became the *Virginia*'s running mate in 1818. Of note, in July 1824, the *Norfolk* had the honor of carrying Revolutionary War hero the Marquis de Lafayette during part of his farewell tour of the United States.

The competition between the various operators on the Baltimore–Norfolk route was intense in the early years, and it became apparent that a company to gather the individual lines into a single entity was desirable. As a result, the Maryland and Virginia Steam Boat Company was formed in March 1828 to bring them all under a single management.

Ferguson's *Virginia* and *Norfolk* were sold at auction and became the first two steamers of the new company. Published schedules provided specific times for departure and arrival and allowed travelers to plan their trips with certainty and make reliable connections. As one boat departed Norfolk, the other left Baltimore and they connected with the steamers on the James River run to Richmond and the Frenchtown route, as well as the offshore line to Charleston, South Carolina. In Baltimore, a steamer left Spear's Wharf every Monday, Wednesday, and Friday at 2 p.m., arriving in Norfolk the next morning.

It did not take the company long to add to the fleet. In 1829, the steamers *Columbus* and *Pocahontas* were built at the Baltimore yard of James Beecham and George Gardiner. They were 137 feet long with a beam of 30 feet and initially operated on a Baltimore–Richmond run with a stop in Norfolk. By 1835, however, they were ending their runs in Norfolk where passengers and freight connected with the steamer *Patrick Henry* for the trip up the James River to Richmond. The veteran *Norfolk*, however, continued to run through to Richmond without stopping in her namesake port.

A few years later, the *Columbus* and *Pocahontas* also called at Lumpkin's Landing in Mathews County, Virginia, adjacent to Mobjack Bay on the western side of the lower Chesapeake. For a time in the late 1830s, steamers of the Maryland and Virginia Steam Boat Company stopped at Harborton in lower Accomack County on Virginia's Eastern Shore on their runs between Baltimore and Norfolk. For the isolated communities on the Virginia Eastern Shore, it was their first regularly scheduled transportation service.

At some point soon after the founding of the new company, the *Virginia* was acquired by the Atlantic Steam Packet Company and was put on its coastal run to Charleston, South Carolina, and Savannah, Georgia. The Maryland and Virginia Steam Boat Company then bought the fast steamer *Kentucky* in 1835 from the People's Steam Navigation Company and it was her speed that turned away several would-be competitors on the Baltimore–Norfolk route. On at least two occasions, the *Kentucky* made the run in just over thirteen hours, considerably faster than any steamers then on the route. Such fast runs proved to be a great attraction for passengers transferring in Norfolk to trains that took them to destinations in North Carolina. Why she did not remain with the company for very long is a mystery. She was listed as abandoned in 1840.

An ever-increasing number of railroads throughout the region about that time meant new competition for both the Maryland and Virginia Steam Boat Company and the Atlantic Steam Packet Company. Despite the competition, both companies continued to operate successfully through most of the 1830s; near the end of the decade, both decided to build new ships.

The Maryland and Virginia Steam Boat Company contracted with W. & G. Gardiner of Baltimore for construction of the steamer *Jewess* and with Levin H. Dunkin of Baltimore for the steamer *Alabama*. The 352-ton *Jewess* was 173 feet long, with a beam of 23 feet. The *Alabama* measured 676 tons and was 210 feet long and 25 feet wide. She was launched on July 24, 1837.

By the time the new boats entered service, the financial picture was rapidly changing. Railroad competition continued to increase, the financial panic of 1837 impacted the company, and the construction costs of the two new boats likely took a financial toll. There was also the company's surprise decision in January 1839 not to renew its contract for carrying the mails because it wanted a payment of $5,000 from the Post Office Department instead of the $3,000 it had been getting—a request that was rejected. In light of the precarious financial picture at that point, it is difficult to understand why the line refused to renew its contract at any price, but it caused considerable consternation. The dispute, however, was eventually settled, but the terms of that settlement have been long lost.

Apparently, the financial picture continued to look grim and the Maryland and Virginia Steam Boat Company decided to end operations in 1840 and sell its steamers *Jewess*, *Pocahontas*, and *Columbus*. The latter steamer was sold for use on a line between Norfolk and Charleston, while the other two were purchased by a new company then being formed—the Baltimore Steam Packet Company. The *Alabama* was not initially acquired by the new company, but joined the fleet in 1841, only to be disposed of later the same year.

Legislation creating the new company was introduced into the Maryland General Assembly in December 1839 and was adopted on March 18, 1840. It took over the assets of the Maryland and Virginia Steam Boat Company with more than sufficient capital to enable it to operate between Baltimore and Norfolk, beginning in the fall of 1840. Two additional steamers were quickly added to the fleet in the summer and fall of 1840—the *South Carolina* and *Georgia* of the Atlantic Steam Packet Company's coastal run to Charleston, then in the midst of liquidation. Both boats had been built in 1836 and had a passenger capacity of about 200. Their masters—James Coffee of the *Georgia* and Thomas Sutton of the *South Carolina*—came over to the new company with their vessels and became favorites of the traveling public.

On October 20, 1840, the Baltimore Steam Packet Company announced that it was operating from the lower end of Spear's Wharf in Baltimore and that its steamers departed daily except Sundays at 9 a.m. for Norfolk and Portsmouth with passengers, freight, and mail, arriving there around 11 p.m. the same day. Passengers would transfer

The *Pocahontas* was one of the first vessels of the company in 1840. There are no known photographs of her.

The Baltimore Steam Packet Company called Spear's Wharf its home in Baltimore harbor for many years. Steamers tied up at the far end of the pier. (*Courtesy of the Maryland Center for History and Culture, #RS9226 CC2851*)

to the train that night to continue their trip south, arriving in Weldon, North Carolina, at 6 a.m. the next day and Wilmington, North Carolina, that evening. Connections could then be made for Charleston and other points south.

A company advertisement of October 20, 1840, stated:

> Passengers will bear in mind that in this line they have no detention, fatigue or annoyance, by changes of baggage, &c., and may rely on the [schedule] above. The Portsmouth and Roanoke Railroad [is] in good order, with cars of modern construction, running on eight wheels with no [freight] cars attached.[2]

The fare all the way to Weldon was $14, including meals on the steamer.

Those steamers bound for Petersburg and Richmond on the company's James River service left Baltimore on Mondays, Wednesdays, and Fridays, with passengers spending the night on board and arriving in Richmond the next afternoon. The fare from Baltimore to Richmond was $10.

By this time, the *Pocahontas* was the oldest vessel in the fleet and had been in service for over a decade, which was a long time for a wooden steamboat in those days. The company promised the traveling public that it would soon add a new steamer with the most modern conveniences, and in the fall of 1841, it signed a contract with the Baltimore shipbuilding firm of Brown & Collyer for the construction of a new wooden-hull sidewheeler 180 feet long with a beam of twenty-three feet. She was to have forty berths in the gentlemen's cabin, which also doubled as the dining saloon. A similar number of berths was found in the ladies' cabin some distance from the men's on another deck. Her name was *Medora* and she would have the shortest career of any Chesapeake Bay steamboat.

Upon completion, the *Medora* was set to depart on her builder's trial run on the afternoon of April 14, 1842, before being officially turned over to the Baltimore Steam Packet Company, and a large crowd turned out in anticipation. Besides shipyard and steamboat company officials, a number of invited guests were aboard bringing the total to seventy-nine for the trial trip. Then, as the steamer began to slowly move, there was a tremendous explosion:

> When the wheels had only made two revolutions, the boiler exploded, throwing the smoke pipes, the forepart of the upper deck and the persons who stood on it, some forty or fifty feet in the air, tearing open the sides of the vessel round the boiler, and scattering fragments of the wood and iron all around, and raising the immense boiler up and throwing it crosswise on the deck.[3]

Clouds of steam enveloped the scene, killing or injuring many of those who had not died outright in the explosion. What was left of the shattered *Medora* sagged to the bottom of the harbor. Twenty-six people were dead, including Andrew F. Henderson, president of the Baltimore Steam Packet Company, and John C. Moale, the company's agent. Thirty-eight were injured and another fifteen who had either been on or near the boat, somehow managed to survive without injury. The cause of the blast was never determined.

Shaken by the accident but undeterred, the Baltimore Steam Packet Company set about salvaging what was left of the *Medora*'s hull, repairing it, installing new machinery, and

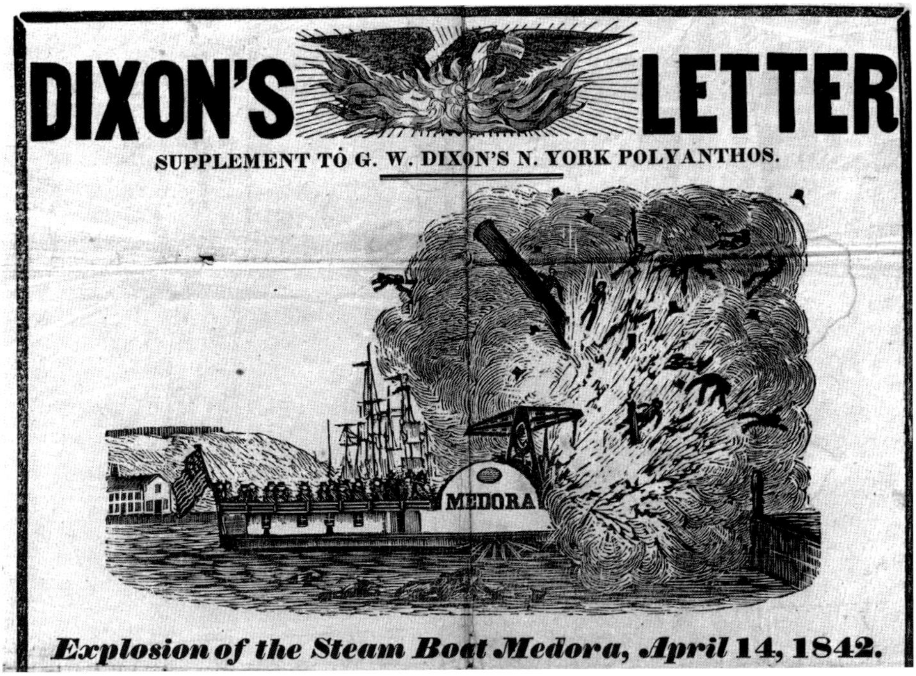

The worst steamboat disaster in Chesapeake Bay history occurred on April 14, 1842, when the company's newest steamer *Medora* exploded at the start of her trial run. (*Courtesy of the Chesapeake Bay Maritime Museum, Dixon's Letter Collection, #0462-0005*)

The *Medora* was rebuilt as the *Herald* and had a long and successful career. She is seen in Baltimore harbor. (*Courtesy of the Chesapeake Bay Maritime Museum, Gift of H.G. Wood, #0000.0958.0006*)

building a new superstructure. By so doing, the company was able to save somewhat on construction costs and at the same time get the new boat into service much quicker than if it had been built new from the keel up. Obviously, the name *Medora* would no longer do, so the new boat was named *Herald* and entered service on October 21, 1842, under the command of Captain George W. Russell.

Once the *Herald* joined the fleet, the *Pocahontas* was used sparingly and operated on a once-a-week trip between Baltimore and Petersburg. In 1845, the aging vessel was sold to the Powhatan Steamboat Company, which had been founded in 1841 to run steamers directly from Baltimore to Richmond and Petersburg. Her consort, *Columbus*, became part of the Powhatan Line at the same time.

The regular boats then in operation between Baltimore and Norfolk were the *Georgia*, *Jewess*, and *Herald*, the *South Carolina* having been disposed of in 1842. For the next several years, operations continued without interruption, and in addition to the Baltimore–Norfolk route, the steamers also made special excursions. Typical was one such excursion on the *Jewess* that began in Baltimore on August 6, 1846. The excursion lasted three days and included stops at Old Point Comfort, Portsmouth, the Norfolk Navy Yard, Yorktown, and a short cruise offshore in the Atlantic.

On January 11, 1848, the *Jewess* was at her Baltimore dock preparing to take on passengers, freight, and mail when fire broke out aboard the steamer *Governor Wolcott*, tied up at the same wharf. Since the *Jewess* did not yet have steam up, and the ice in the harbor was thick, she could not be moved away from the dock before the flames spread to her, according to news reports of the day. The aft end of the steamer and part of the superstructure were completely burned away before she could be scuttled. Another steamer, the *Planter*, was tied up next to the *Jewess*, but was moved away and suffered only minor damage. No one was injured, and the mail was saved, but the *Jewess* was badly damaged.

As it had in the wake of the *Medora* explosion, the company proceeded to raise what was left of the *Jewess* and rebuild her, keeping her name, adding a separate dining saloon, and extending her length to 199 feet at the same time. The *Herald* was also lengthened from 184 feet to 215 feet the same year.

As it approached the mid-point of the nineteenth century following a decade of operation, it was with these two steamers and the veteran *Georgia* that the Baltimore Steam Packet Company looked to the future. Despite the *Medora* explosion and the *Jewess* fire, ambitious plans were in the making.

2

Fleet Expansion and Civil War

The general character of the steamer is promptly acknowledged by many to surpass in almost every respect, any similar vessel of Maryland, and will justify a comparison with even the famed boats of other waters.[1]

The steamer referred to was the *North Carolina* of the Baltimore Steam Packet Company, built in Baltimore by Cooper & Butler with an engine by Murray and Hazelhurst. She had a wooden hull with a length of 239 feet and a beam of 35 feet, and was considerably larger than the *Jewess*, *Herald*, and *Georgia*. As with other wooden hull steamers of the day, she had large wooden hog frames on either side of the deck house to provide greater strength and prevent sagging of the wooden hull. She was said to have been the largest steamer built in Baltimore up to that time and news accounts told of marble-top tables, carved moldings, and polished white paneling in her public rooms. She had accommodations for 200 passengers and could carry 2,000 barrels of freight.

The *North Carolina* entered service in June 1852 and quickly made a name for herself on July 29, 1852, when she steamed from Norfolk to Baltimore in ten hours and five minutes, beating the earlier record by an hour and twenty minutes. However, the regular time allotted for the run was twelve hours, a schedule that remained in effect from that time on. Otherwise, the steamer would be arriving at her destination in the pre-dawn hours. As she was taking her place on the line, the company upgraded the *Georgia* and *Herald*, work that included new boilers and improved staterooms. Pleased with the success of the *North Carolina*, plans were made for a similar running mate that would create a more balanced and up-to-date fleet. With a new and larger steamer on the horizon, the *Jewess* was sold in July 1852.

The contract for the new steamer, to be named *Louisiana*, was also awarded to Cooper & Butler, but this time the engine was built by Charles Reeder & Sons. With a length of 266 feet and a beam of 36 feet, she was bigger than the *North Carolina*. Like her consort, she had a wooden hull and was a sidewheeler, as had been all the boats of the line up to that point. She had sleeping space for about 500 passengers accommodated in several different types of staterooms. Ten rooms with double beds and upper and lower berths were available for use by families. She entered service in late 1854.

With two of the finest inland water steamers in the nation operating between Baltimore and Norfolk, the Bay Line entered an extremely prosperous period in which both passenger

The *Louisiana,* built in 1854, was hailed as one of the most beautiful steamers of her time on the bay. She was very similar to the earlier *North Carolina.* (*Courtesy of the Mariners' Museum and Park, #1949.0509.000001*)

and freight revenues increased. Among the freight being shipped at that time was sugar, molasses, flour, whiskey, china, hollow ware, pig metal, marble, slate, lumber, and bricks. In 1857, the company relocated its Baltimore terminal from Spear's Wharf to Union Dock at the foot of Concord Street, which afforded considerably more space for the storage of freight awaiting shipment and also provided docking space for several vessels. In addition to its regular service, the company continued to offer special cruises from time to time.

Rail connections had improved dramatically over the years, and by the latter part of the 1850s, the company was part of an unofficial rail–water transportation network that offered through tickets between New York, Philadelphia, Baltimore, Norfolk, Weldon, Raleigh, Wilmington, North Carolina, and Charleston, Atlanta, and New Orleans.

Many people from outside the region are surprised to learn that the Chesapeake Bay can freeze, and over the years, heavy ice on numerous occasions significantly affected ship movements. One such case was in January 1857 when it took the *Georgia* fifty-four hours to reach Norfolk from Baltimore. In those days before reliable communications, to have a vessel out of touch for so long caused a great deal of angst. After reaching Norfolk, the *Georgia* did not move again for quite a while. The harbor was so frozen that all ships were forced to remain at their docks for extended periods.

In 1858, the *North Carolina* underwent a major overhaul that included spruced-up accommodations and improved force pumps for fighting fires. No one could have possibly known that within a year those force pumps would be put to the test.

The *North Carolina* departed from Baltimore at the usual time on a rainy January 28, 1859, with twenty-six passengers and forty crew members. It was a routine trip down the bay despite some dense fog. Shortly before 1 a.m., she passed the northbound *Georgia* near the mouth of the Potomac River and continued on, passing the Smith Point Light Ship at about 1:15 a.m. Yet then several miles further on, the night watchman discovered fire in the steward's room forward of the wheelhouse and sounded the alarm.

In 1857, the Old Bay Line relocated its Baltimore terminal to the larger Union Dock at the foot of Concord Street. The two-funneled vessel at the end of the dock is identified as the *Louisiana*, but she had only one funnel. (*Bird's Eye View of Baltimore City by E. Sasche & Co., 1869, Courtesy of the Enoch Pratt Free Library Map Collection*)

Captain James Cannon ordered the force pumps activated and sent crew members through the ship arousing passengers and telling them to be ready to abandon ship if necessary. That it would prove to be necessary was apparent after only a short time as the flames spread rapidly and overwhelmed the force pumps. Fire was the one thing dreaded above all else by the crews and passengers of wooden steamers. Many passengers entered the lifeboats barefoot with only the night clothes they were wearing, and it was through the cool-headed efforts of the crew that they remained calm throughout the ordeal even as the deckhouse was being consumed by flames. At one point, Purser Lloyd Parks ran back into the cabin to see if anyone else was there and returned with blankets to be distributed to passengers. All but two people escaped the burning steamer—a passenger and a young crew member.

Under the direction of Captain Cannon, the lifeboats were gathered together and rowed to the Smith Point Light Ship, where the survivors were given shelter until the steamer *Locust Point* arrived and took them to Old Point Comfort. The *North Carolina* apparently burned down to the waterline and sank but by the time she did so, the survivors were unable to see her end because of the fog. On reaching land, the passengers presented a resolution of thanks to Captain Cannon and his crew for their handling of the disaster.[2]

The Bay Line was stunned by the news. After just seven years in service, one of its grand steamers was gone—a loss that left it with an unbalanced fleet. Initially, the line chartered the one-year-old steamer *George Weems* but she was not as big nor as opulent as the *Louisiana*, so the company set about seeing if the machinery from the *North Carolina* could be salvaged for possible use in a new boat. However, the wintry conditions and the exposed location in the bay near the mouth of the Potomac River confounded those efforts and would-be salvagers were forced to give up. The *North Carolina*'s hulk and her machinery still rest on the bottom of the bay.

When it became apparent that the *North Carolina*'s machinery could not be salvaged, the line succeeded in purchasing the five-year-old *Adelaide* from the Calais Steamboat Company of Maine. The 233-foot steamer was operating at the time on an open ocean route between Boston and New Brunswick, Canada. She was a sturdy 972 gross-ton wooden-hull sidewheeler very similar in size and accommodations to the lost vessel. She arrived in Norfolk in late February and, with the *North Carolina*'s crew aboard, was put

The Maine coastal steamer *Adelaide* was acquired by the company in 1859 to replace the *North Carolina*, which had been destroyed by fire earlier that year. (*Painting by C. Leslie Oursler, courtesy of Susan Bennett*)

on the run to Baltimore one month to the day after the loss of the *North Carolina*. Her arrival once again gave the Bay Line a well-balanced fleet of two large vessels making the nightly run between Baltimore and Norfolk.

Within a year of the *Adelaide*'s addition to the fleet, the company acquired three other vessels—the iron-hull sidewheelers *Georgeanna* and *Philadelphia* and the wooden-hull sidewheel steamer *William Selden*. The *Georgeanna* was 199 feet long with a beam of 30 feet and was built in 1859 in Wilmington, Delaware. She was the company's first iron-hull passenger vessel (the very first iron-hull vessel of the line was the small freighter *Mount Vernon*, which it acquired in 1847). The 201-foot *Philadelphia* was built in Philadelphia for the Seaboard and Roanoke Railroad in 1860 but for some reason only remained with the Bay Line for a year. The 180-foot *William Selden* was built in Washington, D.C. in 1851. This larger fleet enabled the company to offer excursions in addition to its regular run between Baltimore and Norfolk. Perhaps the best known of those excursions occurred in July and August 1860 when the mammoth British liner *Great Eastern* visited Chesapeake Bay.

The 692-foot ship was considerably larger than any other vessel and was considered one of the engineering wonders of the world. She was powered by a combination of screw propeller, paddlewheels, and sails. Her visit to the Chesapeake was one of several such goodwill trips she made along the east coast.

While a number of steamboat companies offered excursions to view the one-of-a-kind ship, only the Bay Line was granted permission for its excursionists to actually board the *Great Eastern*. It had sweetened the pot by giving the ship a thousand tons of coal and, in return, was granted permission for its passengers to not only visit the *Great Eastern*, but to cruise the Chesapeake aboard her. On August 3 and 4, the *Adelaide* and *Louisiana* took 150 passengers down the bay to meet the big liner near Old Point Comfort. She then departed on the trip up the bay to Annapolis Roads at 6 p.m. on August 5 with Bay Line passengers aboard.

She was followed up the bay by an armada of vessels, including steamboats, fishing craft, and private boats, according to contemporary news reports. Among the steamboats were the *William Selden* of the Bay Line and the *George Peabody* of the Powhatan Line. The *Great Eastern* lay at anchor off Annapolis for five days during

The fleet was expanded in 1860 with the acquisition of the *Georgeanna*, the first Old Bay Line steamer with an iron hull. (*Courtesy of The Mariners' Museum and Park, MS0091/03.01-22#0773*)

which time numerous steamboats took the curious to see her, but once again, only the Bay Line's passengers were allowed on board for a tour.

Tensions between south and north were escalating during this period and boiled over following the election of Abraham Lincoln as president and South Carolina's secession from the Union. With the bombardment of Fort Sumter on April 14, 1861, the nation was plunged into a bloody civil war. Although Maryland ultimately remained in the Union, there was considerable southern sentiment in the state and among many of the steamer officers and company personnel. An example of that occurred in the days leading up to the outbreak of war. On April 10, 1861, the *Adelaide* carried pro-southern recruits destined for South Carolina from Baltimore to Norfolk. Just a few days later, the U.S. Navy approached the Bay Line about transporting U.S. naval recruits to the U.S.S. *Pennsylvania* in Norfolk since Virginia was still part of the Union at that time. The company's president, Moor N. Falls, politely but firmly rejected the navy's request.[4]

On May 7, the *Adelaide* arrived at Old Point Comfort from Baltimore on a routine voyage, where Captain Cannon was informed by Flag Officer G. J. Pendergrast, commander of the navy's Home Squadron, that she could land her passengers, freight, and mail there, but could not continue on to Norfolk. Pendergrast said the passengers could not leave Old Point without a permit from him or the commander of Fort Monroe but could not under any circumstances go to Norfolk. The *Adelaide* then headed back to Baltimore and encountered the *Louisiana* near Sharp's Island and informed her master what had happened. Both boats then returned to Baltimore to await a clarification of the issue.

On May 9, official word came from Washington that the Bay Line steamers could operate as far as Old Point Comfort and that a connecting steamer could be provided to take passengers and mail from there to Norfolk. That steamer was the *William Selden*. However, on her first trip as a connecting vessel on May 10, she was captured by Confederate forces in Norfolk, ending the idea of a connecting steamer service. She would never sail again, remaining in Norfolk until she was set afire on May 10, 1862, by the retreating Confederate forces.

Once war officially broke out, the federal authorities set about chartering as many commercial steamers as they could for the blockade of the southeastern coast, and it did not take long for a Bay Line steamer to be taken up for that purpose. The *Adelaide* was chartered by the Union Navy on May 10, 1861, along with the *George Peabody* of the Powhatan Line.

Masts for sails were added to both vessels in the event their engines failed. They each received four 32-lb guns placed at the bow and stern and were assigned a naval armed guard.[5]

Both steamers were to be used as transports for the Atlantic Blockading Squadron. They were part of the fleet sent to wrest control of Hatteras Inlet on the North Carolina Outer Banks from southern forces.[6]

The two steamers carried Union troops from Norfolk to Hatteras Inlet and towed schooners behind them loaded with surf boats to be used in the amphibious landings on August 28 and 29, 1861. The two forts guarding the inlet were captured by the Union forces giving them an entrance into the North Carolina sounds and to Norfolk while also closing the entrance to Confederate blockade runners.[7]

With the *Adelaide* spending most of her time under charter to the Union Navy, the Bay Line looked for a suitable vessel to operate with the *Louisiana*. It acquired the iron steamer *Thomas A. Morgan* from the Delaware River Steamboat Company, but hardly had she arrived in Baltimore in February 1862 than she was chartered by the Union War Department to carry mail between Fort Monroe and Yorktown.

The *Georgia* and *Louisiana* were also used by the federal government at various times, the former carrying troops and the latter carrying prisoners of war to Baltimore. At one point in 1863, the *Georgia* was under government charter for several consecutive months. Even though the federals regained control of Norfolk in May 1862, the bay boats were prevented from going onto the city for the duration of the war, meaning that voyages continued to begin and end at Old Point. All of this played havoc with the company's efforts to maintain a regular nightly service, but it somehow managed to carry on for the duration of the war.

On December 11, 1863 while she was in government service, the *Louisiana* carried Mary Todd Lincoln, the president's wife, from Old Point Comfort on a visit to Baltimore. She was accompanied on the voyage by her mother and two sisters.[8]

Throughout the war, both the passenger and freight business of the Bay Line suffered because the resorts in the Hampton Roads area were closed for the duration, fewer people were traveling, and the southern railroads on which it relied for a significant part of its freight traffic were destroyed. Its vessels had been run hard during the war both in commercial and military service and once hostilities ended, it set about acquiring new tonnage to revitalize the fleet and prepare for the future.

The *Thomas A. Morgan* was purchased in 1862 and was immediately acquired by the U.S. War Department for use in the Hampton Roads area as a mail steamer. (*Courtesy of the Mariners' Museum and Park, #MS0094/01-0733*)

3

The Old Established Bay Line

Once the hostilities ended, the line was allowed to resume service all the way to Norfolk, but passenger traffic was slow to pick up. One reason is that the popular Hotel Hygeia at Old Point Comfort had been demolished during the war and it would be quite some time before a new hotel would be built in the postwar years.[1]

The Bay Line steamers were in need of major overhauls or replacement after their hard work during the war years. For instance, it was not until August 1865 that the *Adelaide* returned to full-time service after a lengthy postwar refit. By that time, the *Georgia* was nearly thirty years old, and it was decided to sell her and move ahead with the construction of a new steamer. That new vessel was the *Thomas Kelso*, named for one of the company's original directors. An iron sidewheeler 237 feet long on a beam of 35 feet, she was built in Chester, Pennsylvania, by Reaney, Son and Company and entered service in early November 1865. She operated on the regular route between Baltimore and Norfolk with the *Louisiana* and *Adelaide*; the *Georgeanna* and *Herald* were held in reserve.

Also, in 1865, the company acquired the 144-foot wooden sidewheeler *Eolus* that was built in 1864 on the Hudson River and was taken up for war service almost immediately and distinguished herself with the North Atlantic Blockading Squadron. Despite her small size, she captured the blockade runner *Hope* in October of that year and assisted in the capture of the British steamer *Lady Stirling*, also a blockade runner. The Bay Line acquired her for passenger and freight feeder operations out of Norfolk and Old Point Comfort. She ran to Yorktown and points in Gloucester and Mathews counties three times a week, as well as across the bay to Cherrystone on Virginia's eastern shore three days a week.[2]

Hardly had the war ended than a competitor appeared on the Baltimore–Norfolk run. Leary and Company, Inc. of New York sent two of its steamers to the Chesapeake to challenge the Bay Line. The company was headed by Thomas Clyde of Philadelphia, who owned or part-owned many steamers along the coast. The *George Leary*, an attractive wooden sidewheeler 237 feet long built for service around New York, and the *James T. Brady*, of similar size, began operating on the Baltimore-Norfolk route on May 22, 1865. They connected at Norfolk with two other Leary steamers—the *Dictator* and *City Point*—running on the James River to Richmond. It did not take long for the competition to heat up and a full-scale rate war was soon in effect. Before long, fares dropped to $1, then 50 cents, 25 cents, and on at least one occasion passengers were briefly carried at no charge.[3]

To emphasize its twenty-five years of service on the Baltimore–Norfolk route, the Baltimore Steam Packet Company began referring to itself as "The Old Established Bay Line" in July 1865. It was eventually shortened to Old Bay Line, the name by which it would be known for nearly 100 years. Leary advertisements referred to its service simply as "The New Line" to differentiate it from the older company. Both lines departed Baltimore and Norfolk at 6:30 p.m. with a stop at Old Point Comfort. Another line, simply referred to as the Peoples' Line, also operated steamers between Baltimore and Richmond for a short time after the war.

A series of mishaps occurred to Leary Line vessels within a short period of time, the first coming on August 25, 1865, when the *George Leary* was rammed off Cove Point by the oceangoing steamer *Seagull*. The *Leary* stayed afloat and took refuge in the nearby Patuxent River. Not long after, following repairs, she rammed and sank a schooner whose entire crew was lost, the *Dictator* was involved in a collision with a tug, and finally the *George Leary* was in collision with the Bay Line's *Louisiana*. Fortunately, the damage to the ships was not serious.

The Bay Line's *Thomas Kelso* had a serious accident of its own on December 8, 1866, when an explosion rocked the steamer near Wolf Trap Light about halfway down the bay from Baltimore. Five crew members, all engineering personnel including the chief engineer, were killed and a number of other crew members and passengers were badly scalded. She was towed to Portsmouth, Virginia, for repairs.[4]

Perhaps because of the rash of accidents it had experienced in such a short time or the tough competition from the Old Bay Line, the Leary Line sold out to the older company in January 1867. Under terms of the transaction, the *George Leary* was added to the Bay Line's Baltimore–Norfolk fleet. The other boats that Leary had run on the Chesapeake and James River returned to the company's home base in New York. However, Thomas Clyde was not through on Chesapeake Bay.

The year 1867 also saw several other changes in the Old Bay Line fleet. The *Herald*, by then twenty-five years old, was sold to new owners on the Hudson River where she ran until 1885. It was also the year the line obtained the *New Jersey*, its first propeller-driven vessel, and also its first freight-only vessel. She was acquired as part of a trade-in involving the *Thomas A. Morgan*. A second freighter, the *Transit*, followed in 1869, the same year that the Old Bay Line disposed of the *Eolus*, *Georgeanna*, and *Thomas Kelso*. The sale of the four-year-old *Thomas Kelso* seems strange given her newness, but off she went to new owners to be registered in Providence, Rhode Island. Following these transactions, the Bay Line's passenger fleet consisted of the *George Leary*, *Louisiana*, and *Adelaide*.[5]

A close relationship that the Baltimore Steam Packet Company had with the Seaboard & Roanoke Railroad prior to the Civil War became closer in the years following the war. In 1867, John M. Robinson became president of both the Bay Line and the railroad and had headquarters in Baltimore. At first, the Bay Line owned the railroad, but over time, the railroad eventually grew into the Seaboard Air Line Railway and it eventually acquired control of the steamboat company. That ownership would continue in part until 1962.[6]

Fire, which had been a nemesis of the Bay Line from its earliest years, struck the company again on February 26, 1870. The *New Jersey* sailed from Baltimore for Norfolk the previous afternoon with a heavy load of freight estimated at 750 tons with a value of about $40,000. It was 12:30 a.m. as she was steaming past the Sharps Island Light near the mouth of the Choptank River, when fire broke out amidships on the freight deck.[7]

Despite the efforts of the crew to fight the fire, it quickly gained a foothold, forcing the eleven-man crew to take to the boats and watch helplessly as their ship blazed furiously. Efforts by the rescue tug *Pacific* to push the burning steamer onto the nearby flats failed and what was left of the *New Jersey* sank at 10 a.m. The burned steamer's remains and what was left of her freight lay undisturbed in the dark waters of the bay until 1975 when it was rediscovered and became the subject of high-technology underwater archaeology, the results of which had a long-lasting impact (See *Ghost Fleet of Mallows Bay* by Donald G. Shomette).

Events began unfolding in 1873 that would affect the Old Bay Line for many years to come. The Richmond and York River Railroad, which connected the steamers of the Powhatan Steamboat Company at West Point, Virginia, with Richmond, was in financial trouble. It was sold at auction on May 2, 1873, to the same Thomas Clyde, who had operated the Leary Line, and other investors. Under the new owners and their substantial financial resources, the line was renamed the Richmond, York River and Chesapeake Railroad and made Reuben Foster of Baltimore its agent. He would play a major role in the Chesapeake Bay steamboat industry for years to come.

That same year, the railroad took over the Powhatan Line and its operations between Baltimore and West Point and purchased the steamer *Sue* for that run. She also ran several days a week to Richmond and Petersburg. The *Sue* had previously been operated by the Eastern Shore Steamboat Company. The new company that was formed to operate the York River line was named the Baltimore, Chesapeake and Richmond Steamboat Company and began operations on February 1, 1874, with Reuben Foster now as general manager.[8]

In addition to the *Sue*, the new company began operations with the sidewheelers *Louise* and *Havana* and the screw-propelled *E.C. Biddle* and *Empire*. It later added the *John S. Ide* and *Lucille*. The *Louise*, built in 1864, would have one of the longest careers of any bay steamer, lasting until 1933. Eventually, through a series of complex transactions, the Baltimore, Chesapeake and Richmond Steamboat Company came under the ownership of the Southern Railway. Initially it was content to run steamers between Baltimore and West Point on the York River, which was then the freight terminal of the Southern Railway, but that would soon change.

The year 1874 was not a good one for the Old Bay Line. It was extremely concerned about the effect the new opposition York River line would have on its freight operations on the James River to Richmond, and then on November 14 disaster befell the *Louisiana*. She was headed up the bay to Baltimore in clear weather with 112 people aboard, fifty-six of whom were passengers, when she collided with the Charleston-bound steamer *Falcon* near Smith Point at the mouth of the Potomac River. The *Louisiana* was rammed dead amidships on the port side, opening a huge gash in her side.

Captain Wyndham R. Mayo hoped at first that he could beach the ship in nearby shallow water but the engine was jammed and she was unable to move. A line was run over to the *Falcon* in the hope that she could tow the *Louisiana* to shoal water, but the steamer had taken on so much water that a tow was ruled out. There was, however, time to transfer all passengers, their baggage, the mails, and even some of the furniture from the public rooms. After forty-five minutes, the *Louisiana* went down, leaving her

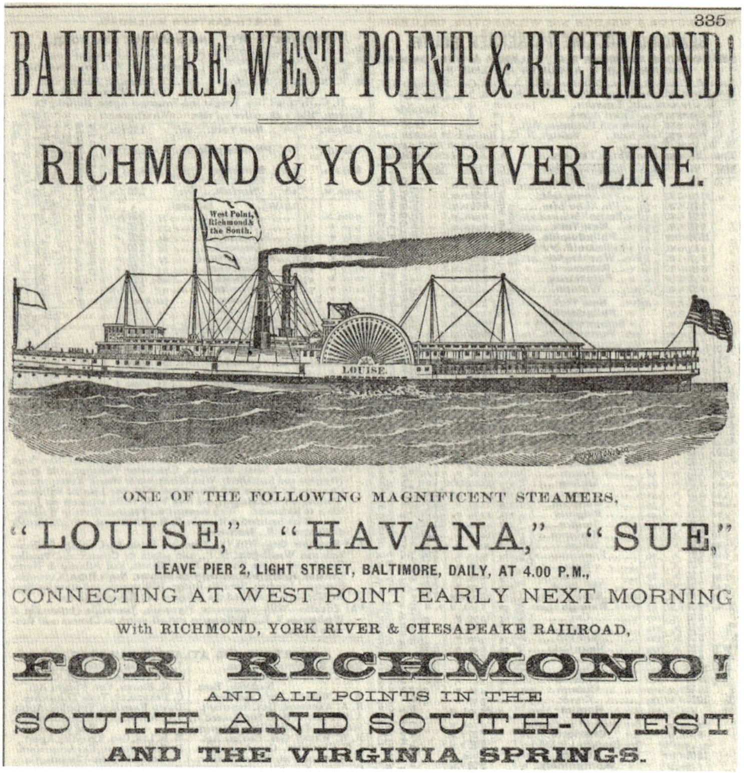

Left: An early advertisement for the Richmond and York River Line, which became known as the Baltimore, Chesapeake and Richmond Steamboat Company, operating passenger and freight steamers between Baltimore and York River points.

Below: The small sidewheeler *Sue* was one of the first steamers on the Baltimore, Chesapeake, and Richmond Steamboat Company's Baltimore–West Point run in 1874.

funnel, pilothouse, and part of the upper deck above water. There were no fatalities. As to what caused the crash, that was a mystery because both ships had sighted each other and exchanged whistle signals. Captain Mayo was perplexed, saying there was more than ample room for both vessels to safely pass each other. Ultimately, it was concluded that a mix-up in whistle signals was likely to blame.[9]

The collision left the Old Bay Line with only two first-class steamers suited for its Baltimore–Norfolk service—the *George Leary* and *Adelaide*. It was always desirable to have three vessels so one could be held as a spare and used whenever the need arose. The situation called for a complete overhauling of the fleet, but it was not until 1876 that the first step in that direction could be taken.

The sidewheeler *Florida*, 259 feet in length and 36 feet wide, was built in Baltimore by Wm. Skinner & Son in 1876. She was the last wooden-hull vessel built for the company, and although she proved somewhat difficult to handle, the general consensus is that she was the most elegant steamer to ever sail the bay with such features as a skylight the length of the grand saloon, a variety of hard woods, gleaming brass, and ornate gas lighting fixtures.[10]

A new vessel was always a major attraction so the timing of the new ship's arrival was fortunate for the Old Bay Line inasmuch as competition was about to appear. That same year, the Baltimore, Chesapeake and Richmond Steamboat Company decided to start a line of passenger and freight steamers between Baltimore and Norfolk in direct opposition to the Old Bay Line to take advantage of the deep-water terminals in Norfolk. Two steamers were assigned to that route, which operated every day except Sunday. It was known simply as "The Peoples' Line" and its entry into the Baltimore–Norfolk trade immediately triggered a rate war with the Bay Line that saw passenger fares and freight rates drop precipitously.

Rather than have rock-bottom rates adversely affect revenues, the two lines quickly realized that they had to work together. Under a compromise reached in January 1877, the Old Bay Line agreed to discontinue any business it had on the York and James Rivers and sold its freighter *Shirley*. The Baltimore, Chesapeake and Richmond Steamboat Company, for its part, ended its Baltimore–Norfolk service and turned over several feeder lines in North Carolina to the Bay Line. The agreement was to be in force for five years, and it carried with it a financial penalty if either party violated it.

The *Florida* of 1876 was considered the most elegant steamer ever to sail the Chesapeake Bay with interior decorations reportedly unmatched by any other Chesapeake vessel. She was also the Bay Line's last wooden hull vessel. (*Painting by C. Leslie Oursler*)

The new *Florida* proved to be a fast and dependable steamer even though she could be difficult to steer. She was followed in 1877 by the iron-hull sidewheeler *Carolina*, built by Harlan and Hollingsworth in Wilmington, Delaware. An extremely sturdy vessel, she was 251 feet long, 35 feet wide, and was powered by the engine that had been salvaged from the wreck of the *Louisiana*. She could do 17 miles per hour. In 1879, the Bay Line completed its fleet replacement with the introduction of the *Virginia*, sister ship to the *Carolina*.

With three new nearly identical steamers, the Old Bay Line sold the *George Leary* and *Adelaide* and looked ahead with confidence. For some years, an alliance had been formed with the Seaboard and Roanoke Railroad for the shipment of freight north to Baltimore. That company eventually morphed into the Seaboard Air Line Railway, which extended its reach—and by extension the Bay Line's reach—into the Deep South.

The early 1880s witnessed the beginning of what is widely regarded as the heyday of the steamboat on Chesapeake Bay. Not only were vessels running between Baltimore and Norfolk and Baltimore and Richmond but also to many small town and country wharves on the bay and its tributaries. There were more than 300 landings on both sides of the bay and its rivers that saw Baltimore-based passenger and freight steamboats practically every day of the year for decades. The steamboat was the lifeline for the residents, farms, and businesses in those rural areas. There were steamers out of Norfolk too, although not as many, because much of the steamboat business on the Chesapeake was based in Baltimore. It is not surprising then, that many new steamers were introduced during the 1880s and beyond. Historian David C. Holly referred to it as a pageant of steamboats.[11]

In 1883, the Baltimore, Chesapeake and Richmond Steamboat Company built the first of several new boats that both lines would construct well into the second decade of the twentieth century. The wooden hull *Danville* was built in Baltimore by William E. Woodall and Company. She was 228 feet long with a beam of 35 feet and could carry 150 passengers as well as freight. Her design was somewhat unusual in that her wooden hull was shaped more like that of an oceangoing steamer than a bay steamer's hull and its overhanging guards. She made her first voyage between Baltimore and West Point on January 4, 1883. The *Danville* was the first of four similar steamers that were built for the company between 1883 and 1896. She was joined in August 1885 by the *Baltimore*, also of wood, with a length of 236 feet and a beam of 38 feet. The third in this class of similar York River steamers was to follow in 1889 with the launching of the iron-hulled *Charlotte*.

A passenger and freight steamer built for the Old Bay Line in 1887 was notable for several reasons—she was the largest vessel yet owned by the line, was its first iron hull passenger ship, and introduced an exterior design that became the model for just about every steamer that followed her. The *Georgia*, built by Harlan and Hollingsworth, was 280 feet long, and 40 feet wide. She had a classic profile that for many observers qualified her as the most handsome vessel having sailed the Bay up to that time. She had steam heat in her staterooms, electric lights, brass railings, deep pile carpet and more. When the *Georgia* joined the fleet, she operated alongside the *Carolina* and *Virginia*, the *Florida* becoming the spare boat.[12]

As it entered the decade of the 1890s, the Old Bay Line was in solid financial condition and was looking ahead toward the new century with confidence.

The *Virginia* of 1879 was the company's last sidewheeler and was known for her speed. She was a sister of the *Carolina*. (*Painting by C. Leslie Oursler, courtesy of Susan Bennett*)

This image of the *Florida* is a detail section from a nineteenth-century lithograph showing her at Old Point Comfort next to the Hotel Hygiea. (*Courtesy of the Mariners' Museum and Park, #1964.0143.000001*)

The *Danville* was the first of four similar steamers built for the Baltimore, Chesapeake, and Richmond Steamboat Company between 1883 and 1896. The power plant at left with the four smokestacks is the only thing in this image that still exists. (*I&M Oppenheimer postcard*)

Built in 1887, the *Georgia* was the line's first propeller-driven passenger vessel and had a graceful profile that was the model for most of the Chesapeake Bay steamboats that followed her. (*Courtesy of the Maryland Center for History and Culture, MC10037*)

Following a career of only sixteen years with the Bay Line, the iron-hull *Carolina* had a long life in Canada under the names *Murray Bay* and *Cape Diamond*, operating on the St. Lawrence River. She remained in service until 1933.

4

Intense Competition

The 1890s and early 1900s saw more steamboats on Chesapeake Bay than at any other time in the long history of the industry. Fleets were constantly being updated or replaced, business was booming, more people were traveling than ever before, and there was real reason for optimism for the years ahead. Unfortunately for the Old Bay Line, the new decade began on a negative note.

On the night of July 28, 1890, the *Virginia* was making her way down the outer reaches of Baltimore harbor in clear weather bound for Norfolk when she collided with the inbound Tolchester Line excursion steamer *Louise*. The *Virginia* had sighted a schooner ahead of her and altered course to give it a wide berth when the *Louise* came into view behind the schooner. Whistle signals indicated course changes to be taken, but the schooner was in such a position that the *Virginia* could not maneuver properly and she plowed into the starboard side of the heavily laden excursion steamer.[1]

Panic broke out among the estimated 1,400 people on the *Louise*, but she was not in danger of sinking despite the big hole in her side and was able to make port under her own steam. The *Virginia*'s bow was damaged but she also was in no danger of sinking. Fourteen people on the *Louise* lost their lives in the collision.

After the *Georgia* had been in service for some time, it was decided to build a similar steamer to once again give the company a balanced fleet of modern vessels for its Baltimore–Norfolk line. The Maryland Steel Company at Sparrows Point, Maryland, was awarded a contract in 1892 for construction of the steel-hull *Alabama*, a larger and faster version of the *Georgia*. At 293 feet, she was the largest steamer the Bay Line had yet owned. With the *Alabama* slated to enter service in early 1893, the Old Bay Line retired the *Florida*. She was sold for scrap soon after but sank on the way to the scrapyard.

More misfortune befell the Old Bay Line on June 14, 1892, when a fire tore through its Union Dock complex in Baltimore, destroying not only the wooden buildings, but thousands of dollars' worth of freight awaiting shipment. The fire broke out among hundreds of bales of cotton and spread rapidly to the surrounding sheds and a wide variety of freight including hogsheads of tobacco, bags of flour, barrels of whiskey, rosin, and much more.

Above left: The main staircase on the *Alabama* was surmounted by a large mirror underneath which was the vessel's builder's nameplate.

Above right: Looking forward on the saloon deck of the *Alabama* (third deck above the waterline). Stateroom doors line both sides of the lounge.

This is a typical bedroom aboard the *Alabama*. To the right in the netting is a rolled-up blanket bearing the initials "BSPC" (Baltimore Steam Packet Company).

Two steamers were at the pier when the blaze erupted—the *Carolina* was docked at the end of the pier complex and was so close to where the fire broke out that the paint on her bow blistered. Since she did not have steam up, she was pulled away from the danger by three tugs. The freighter *Gaston*, which had arrived earlier in the day, was on the west side of the pier, and was able to safely back away under her own steam. Both vessels were able to sail that night. Overall damage from the fire was estimated at $250,000. Until Union Dock could be rebuilt, the Bay Line steamers moved to a temporary location on Light Street.[2]

The *Alabama* joined the fleet in April 1893 and was immediately hailed as the queen of Chesapeake Bay steamers. Much was made of the red oak joiner work in her interior, the white and gold paneling with cherry trim, and her mahogany staircases with brass facings. She had a freight capacity of 750 tons and was a fast boat and eclipsed the fastest running time of the *Georgia* by steaming to Norfolk at a speed of more than 19 miles per hour. With the addition of the *Alabama* to the fleet, it decided to retain the *Virginia* as the spare boat and sell the *Carolina*, which went on to a long career in Canadian waters, lasting until 1933.

By 1894, the Southern Railway had succeeded the Thomas Clyde interests as owner of the Baltimore, Chesapeake and Richmond Steamboat Company and was making ambitious plans. The Southern itself was controlled by J. Pierpont Morgan and Company, which felt that since Thomas Clyde was no longer in the picture, the five-year no-compete agreement he had signed with the Old Bay Line back in 1877 was no longer in force. The Southern then announced plans to move its primary steamer terminals for through freight from West Point to Norfolk—a move that would put it in direct competition with the Old Bay Line.

The management of the Old Bay Line was stunned and made no secret of its displeasure. A series of letters flew back and forth between its president, Richard Curzon Hoffman, Southern Railway's president, Samuel Spencer, and Baltimore, Chesapeake and Richmond Steamboat Company's president, Reuben Foster, in which the Bay Line protested the planned move. At first, in an attempt to keep the peace, the Bay Line offered to handle the Southern's traffic through Norfolk itself but the railroad was against such a proposition. Hoffman described the proposed switch of main terminals "uncalled for."[3]

In a face-to-face meeting with Foster on August 27, 1895, Hoffman called it "an unnecessary attack on the Baltimore Steam Packet Company, which was the old established line between Baltimore and Norfolk, and that must be the reason for the attack." He also said he did not believe there was enough business for two lines operating on the same route. "I could see nothing but trouble in this matter," Hoffman said. Foster's response was that the only solution was a compromise in which the Southern and the Atlantic Coast Line railroad acquired an interest in the Bay Line.[4]

Hoffman dismissed that idea and remained steadfast in his opposition to the proposed new line, saying that it could lead to "a thorough demoralization of rates from Richmond north, and I do not see what can be gained from doing the business from Baltimore by a much longer route via Norfolk than over the shorter route via West Point." The Southern's Spencer believed the answer was a consolidation of the Old Bay Line and the Baltimore, Chesapeake and Richmond Steamboat Company.

Hoffman rejected that idea even as his competitor went ahead and started its new Baltimore–Norfolk line. He said that "the conclusion is inevitable that the intruders

Left: It was common practice for steamboat lines and railroads to issue passes to certain individuals to give them free passage. Many of those passes were quite colorful.

Below: In the first decade of the twentieth century, the Old Bay Line had three outstanding similar steamers in service. The *Alabama* of 1893 was the company's first steel hull steamer. The *Virginia* of 1905 and the *Florida* of 1907 were near sister ships similar to the *Alabama*'s design.

Above left: Old Bay Line President Richard Curzon Hoffman fought to keep the Baltimore, Chesapeake, and Richmond Steamboat Company from entering the Baltimore–Norfolk trade in opposition to the Bay Line. (*Courtesy of The Maryland Club*)

Above right: Reuben Foster was president of the Baltimore, Chesapeake, and Richmond Steamboat Company when it entered the Baltimore–Norfolk trade in competition with the Old Bay Line. (*Courtesy of John W.S. Foster*)

upon our domain intend by systematic attacks upon the Bay Line to demoralize its revenues and inflict on it all the injury possible, to break it down or drive it from the sea."[5]

The Baltimore, Chesapeake and Richmond Steamboat Company began its new Norfolk service known as the Peoples' Line on July 1, 1896, with the steamers *Atlanta* and *Charlotte* on a schedule that exactly paralleled that of the Old Bay Line. The *Atlanta,* the fourth of the newbuilding program that began in 1885, had entered service only days before, and it did not take long for the feared rate war to begin with both lines dramatically slashing both freight and passenger rates.

Now that the new Norfolk line was in operation, the Old Bay Line acted swiftly in announcing that, in retaliation, it would initiate an all-water route between Baltimore and Richmond with no stop in Norfolk to oppose its rival's water-rail route to Richmond by way of West Point. Although the main terminal was now at Norfolk, regularly scheduled steamer and train service between Baltimore and Richmond by way of West Point continued for the Baltimore, Chesapeake and Richmond Steamboat Company.

The wooden hull *Baltimore* was built in 1885, the second of four similar vessels added to the fleet of the Baltimore, Chesapeake, and Richmond Steamboat Company.

Just sixteen days after the start of the new Baltimore–Norfolk line, the Old Bay Line opened its own James River passenger-freight service with the sidewheeler *Virginia*, which had been serving as the company's reserve steamer. The *Virginia*, said to be the largest sidewheeler to go up the James, found the going difficult but managed to make Richmond on July 18. On her return trip, however, she ran hard aground in the upper river and remained stuck for some time, forcing the Bay Line to suspend its James River service after only half a voyage.[6]

Meantime, the rate war was in full swing on both the Baltimore–Norfolk route and the York River route. Old Bay Line passenger rates dipped to $1 one way and $1.50 for a round trip. Once the *Virginia* returned to service, the company announced that all shipments to Richmond by way of its James River line would be delivered free to consignees in Richmond. The Baltimore, Chesapeake and Richmond Steamboat Company had no choice but to match those rates. In September 1896, the Old Bay Line took another approach in opposing the rival Norfolk line. It sued the Baltimore, Chesapeake and Richmond Steamboat Company for allegedly violating the agreement of 1877. One must remember, however, that the agreement between the two companies was to have been in force for only five years, and it was now thirteen years since it expired.

The Baltimore Steam Packet Company decided that if the Baltimore, Chesapeake and Richmond Steamboat Company was going to remain on the Norfolk route, it would have to take steps to provide permanent and reliable service on its Baltimore–Richmond route. When it became apparent that the *Virginia* was ill-suited to operate on a river like the James, the Bay Line contracted with Harlan and Hollingsworth for a smaller, more maneuverable twin-screw vessel named *Tennessee* that would be able to better navigate the twisting river.

It was clear that the rate war was hurting both lines, and on December 9, 1897, they issued a joint statement that ended it, saying they had agreed to co-operate with each other in an amicable fashion. The timing could not have been better because there

The *Tennessee*, built in 1898, was the company's only twin-screw vessel and was intended for a run from Baltimore to Richmond by way of the James River.

was widespread concern that the dispute was having a negative impact on all freight movement in the south. The suit referred to earlier apparently never proceeded very far as a result of the agreement.[7]

As part of the rate settlement, the Old Bay Line gave up its direct Baltimore–Richmond service, and the *Virginia* reverted to her former role as reserve steamer. The new 245-foot Old Bay Line steamer *Tennessee* was completed after the agreement was reached and never had the chance to show what she could do on the James River. Being so much smaller than the regular boats, she mostly served as a standby for the regular vessels until March 1906 when she was sold to the Joy Steamship Company for service on Long Island Sound.

On May 17, 1898, fire again reared its ugly head. Only six years after its Union Dock facilities had been destroyed by fire, the company's rebuilt terminal at that location was the scene of another huge fire. Once again, the large freight sheds and a huge quantity of freight was heavily damaged. The blaze, which was believed to have been started by spontaneous combustion, threatened the *Alabama* as she lay alongside without steam up. Fortunately, the company tugboat *Elsie* was able to pull her away from the pier, but not before much of the paint on the starboard side was blistered by the heat. Damage to the pier complex was put at $100,000.

Since property was available at Pier Ten, Light Street, the Bay Line operations were diverted to that location on what initially was a temporary basis. As it turned out, the line permanently acquired the property and continued its operations from Pier Ten for the next fifty-two years.

The twentieth century began with a number of developments involving Baltimore-Norfolk steamboat operations. On January 25, 1900, the Chesapeake Steamship Company was incorporated and acquired the operations of the Baltimore, Chesapeake and Richmond Steamboat Company. Reuben Foster continued as general manager. The new company's Baltimore-Norfolk service was known as the Chesapeake Line and its operation to West Point, Virginia, was known as the York River Line.

Following a disastrous fire at Union Dock, the Old Bay Line moved to Pier Ten, Light Street, and built this imposing terminal, which it used for more than fifty years. (*Leighton & Valentine Co. of New York*)

The Bay Line's Norfolk pier was at the foot of Main Street in the heart of the business district. It served until 1962. Either the *Virginia* of 1905 or the *Florida* of 1907 is alongside. (*Illustrated Postcard Company*)

Old Point Comfort as it appeared around 1900 with the first Hotel Chamberlin, built in 1896, overlooking Government Dock, where the Old Bay Line steamers docked. (*Detroit Publishing Company postcard*)

The Seaboard Air Line Railway completely acquired the Old Bay Line at about this time so that it would have a connection to the Baltimore freight market and beyond since its rails didn't physically touch the city. Under Seaboard ownership, the Bay Line continued to operate as an independent entity although there would be a single president of both companies for many years. Already partly owned by the Southern Railway, the Chesapeake Line would also come under partial ownership by the Atlantic Coast Line.

A flurry of new steamboat construction began in 1900 and over the next thirteen years, eight steamers would be built by the two companies, all but two for the Baltimore–Norfolk run. First out of the gate was the Chesapeake Line's *Augusta*, built by Neafie & Levy Ship and Engine Building Company of Philadelphia. She was a steel hull vessel 245 feet in length with a beam of 46 feet and a gross tonnage of 2,372. She was notable in that she sported two unusually tall funnels, the tops of which were 84 feet above her boiler room. Her interiors featured mahogany, quartered oak, and a carved hardwood main staircase. She is also believed to have been the first steamer on the bay with brass bedsteads. She entered service on the Baltimore–Norfolk run and was paired with the *Atlanta* of 1896. A new boat always proved popular and the *Augusta* was no exception, which prompted the Baltimore Steam Packet Company to once again promote its longevity by referring to itself in advertisements as the "Old and Reliable Bay Line."[8]

A handsome new steamer built by Harlan and Hollingsworth was added to the Bay Line in 1905. She was named *Virginia*, the old sidewheeler of the same name having been sold several years earlier. She was 296 feet long with a beam of 44 feet and was placed in service with the slightly smaller *Alabama*, the *Georgia* being relegated to spare steamer status. Once the *Virginia* had proven totally satisfactory in service, the company turned to the Maryland Steel Company at Sparrows Point, Maryland in 1907 for a similar running mate. Although at first glance they looked like identical sisters, the new *Florida* was

Above left: In 1900, the Baltimore, Chesapeake, and Richmond Steamboat became the Chesapeake Steamship Company and operated two lines: the Chesapeake Line between Baltimore and Norfolk and the York River Line between Baltimore and West Point, Virginia.

Above right: The Chesapeake Line's first brand new steamer was the twin-stack *Augusta* built in 1900 to run opposite the Bay Line's *Alabama.*

Above left: The Old Bay Line built the 296-foot *Virginia* in 1905 to compete with the Chesapeake Line's *Augusta* of 1900. The *Virginia* was, for a time, the largest steamer on the bay. (*Louis Kaufmann & Sons postcard*)

Above right: Looking down the length of the *Virginia*'s gallery deck. The stairway in the foreground leads to the saloon deck.

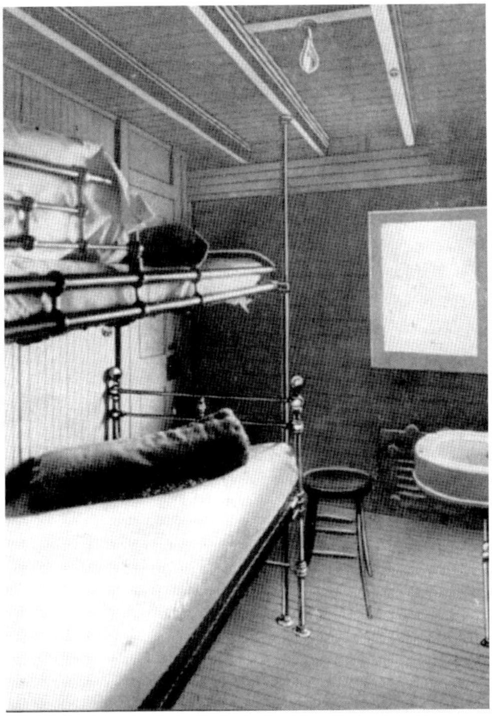

Above left: A typical two-person stateroom on the *Virginia* with upper and lower berths and a sink with hot and cold running water, which was a fairly new attraction at the time.

Above right: Bedrooms on the *Virginia* included both a private shower and tub.

slightly larger than the *Virginia*. She had 136 staterooms to her running mate's 110 rooms, but additional staterooms were later added to the *Virginia* and the *Alabama*.

At about the same time that the *Florida* entered service, the Chesapeake Line introduced its newest vessel, the *Columbia*, a product of the New York Shipbuilding Corporation in Camden, New Jersey. She was 269 feet long with a beam of 46 feet and a gross tonnage of 2,582. Her single funnel was unusually tall like the two on the *Augusta* and her contract speed was 19 miles per hour. All staterooms on the *Columbia* were outside rooms.

A major source of traffic for both lines was the Jamestown Exposition commemorating the 300th anniversary of the Jamestown settlement. It ran from April 26 to December 1, 1907, and with thousands of people flocking to the event, both lines ran day and night steamers to handle the passenger load. The overnight steamers maintained their usual schedule with a 6:30 p.m. departure, while the day boats left Baltimore at 7:30 a.m., calling at Old Point Comfort at 6:30 p.m. and Norfolk at 7:30 p.m. It was during this period of heavy traffic that several unofficial races took place between the *Virginia* and *Columbia* to see which steamer was the fastest on the bay. The outcome was always in dispute, but the matter was finally resolved when the *Florida* entered service. Her contract called for a service speed of 16 miles per hour, but she turned out to be capable of 21 miles per hour when additional speed was required.

A near-sister to the *Virginia,* the *Florida* came out in 1907 and offered similar amenities. She had 136 staterooms and was the largest steamer south of New York. She is seen here fitting out at the yard of the Maryland Steel Company, where she was built.

The smoking room on the *Florida,* located near the stern on the main deck, also doubled as the entrance foyer where passengers were welcomed aboard by the purser.

Passengers gather on the covered after end of the *Florida*'s gallery or saloon deck—a good place to take in the sights during the voyage.

On October 1, 1909, Reuben Foster resigned as president of the Chesapeake Steamship Company, ending an active career in Chesapeake Bay steamboating that went back forty-one years. During his long tenure, both passenger and freight revenue increased dramatically. He was succeeded by Key Compton, the company's vice president. Compton began his career in 1885 in a number of positions before becoming general freight and passenger agent for the Old Bay Line. The freight and passenger business was brisk for both lines at that time, prompting Old Bay Line President John R. Sherwood to say that the time was right to expand to a seven-day-a-week operation by adding Sunday sailings, for the first time in the company's history.[9]

Compton had been president of the Chesapeake Line a little more than six months when he announced in March 1910 plans to build two identical landmark steamers for the Baltimore–Norfolk run. The steamers—to be named *City of Baltimore* and *City of Norfolk*—would be the largest and finest vessels ever turned out for Chesapeake Bay service. They were 310 feet in length overall and 60 feet over guards and could carry 400 passengers and 650 tons of freight. There were 137 inside and outside staterooms. They had one more deck than other bay boats, which put the wheelhouse on the hurricane deck three decks above the main, or freight, deck.[10]

A major innovation of the vessels was placing their dining rooms at the forward end of the gallery deck, where most wheelhouses had previously been located, to give diners a view of the passing scenery and landmarks. From an operational point of view, identical ships made it easier to transfer engine and deck personnel from vessel to vessel without having to familiarize themselves with ships of different designs. Passenger agents and others on the passenger side of the business benefitted from dealing with accommodations of identical design.[11]

Both ships were built by the Maryland Steel Company at Sparrows Point, Maryland and were launched in a double ceremony on December 3, 1910. Each had cost $375,000—a considerable sum for that time. Following fitting out, the *City of Baltimore* made her maiden voyage to Norfolk on April 13, 1911 with the *City of Norfolk* following soon after.[12] They were widely praised in industry journals, with *International Marine Engineering* stating

The sister ships *City of Baltimore* and *City of Norfolk* of the Chesapeake Line were built side-by-side at Sparrows Point. A major attraction was the location of their dining rooms all the way forward on the gallery deck. The pilothouse was relocated one deck above the dining room. (*Courtesy of the Maryland Center for History and Culture SVF*)

in its August 1911 issue that they "are among the finest examples of the luxury to which the traveling custom is becoming accustomed and demanding." It described the passenger accommodations as "most elaborate." As it turned out, one of the sister ships would survive long enough to be the last active night boat in the United States.[12]

The new steamers naturally attracted a large number of travelers and business was very good for the Chesapeake Line's Baltimore–Norfolk run. A spirited competition continued with the Old Bay Line, which had its own nearly new fleet of vessels and advertised them as "the finest steamers south of New York" operating on a "popular and pleasant route."[13]

The Chesapeake Line, however, was not finished modernizing its fleet. Business on its York River Line was flourishing and the boats were running full. The steamers *Atlanta* and *Charlotte* had been on that route since 1907 but were proving less than adequate given the increase in business. To address the situation in the short term, the *Columbia* of 1907 was put on the route and the *Atlanta* became the spare boat. Only seventeen months after its big new Norfolk steamers went into service, the Chesapeake Line announced that it was building a similar, though smaller, pair of identical boats for the York River Line. They were the *City of Richmond* and *City of Annapolis*, each 261 feet in length with a beam of 53 feet and a capacity of 400 passengers and 550 tons of freight. Their passenger accommodation was the same as the larger sisters because they had cabins on the hurricane deck behind the wheelhouse and the earlier two boats did not.

They were also launched in a double ceremony at Sparrows Point on May 31, 1913. Christening the *City of Richmond* was Anne Carter Lee, granddaughter of General Robert E. Lee. Both vessels were well-received by the traveling public as well as *International Marine Engineering*, which stated in its January 1914 issue that they were "classed among the finest and most modern on the run out of Baltimore."[14]

The addition of new vessels meant that the *Charlotte*, *Baltimore*, and *Danville* were sold to new owners in New England. That left, in addition to the four new steamers, the *Atlanta* and *Augusta*, but they did not last much longer either. In 1916, they were sold to new owners, the *Augusta* being converted into a freighter, the *Atlanta* eventually going to Long

Above: The two sisters had very attractive profiles. They proved so popular that more staterooms were added on the top deck behind the pilothouse in 1922. This is the *City of Baltimore*. One of them would survive to become the very last overnight passenger and freight steamer in the U.S.

Right: The Old Bay Line went to great lengths to promote its near-sister ships in the face of the competition from the big new Chesapeake Line steamers. This attractive advertisement is from 1912.

Island Sound. The *Columbia* remained as the spare boat, but underwent a major renovation that also gave her an extra deck, a dining room forward on the gallery deck, and a profile that closely resembled the line's four newest ships. She was later named *City of Atlanta*.

In the middle of all these fleet changes, misfortune came to one of the new steamers. The *City of Richmond* was tied up at West Point on June 14, 1915, when she sank alongside the pier in 22 feet of water. No passengers were aboard at the time, and it was believed that with the up and down movements of the tide, her guard rail caught under the pier, and she listed and took on water. Why none of the crew members aboard at the time noticed this is unclear. She was raised in short order, however, repaired, and put back in service later that year.[15]

When the United States entered World War I, the freight and passenger business increased dramatically because Hampton Roads was a port of embarkation, home to a number of military facilities and a bustling commercial port. Steamers had to contend with submarine nets in certain locations in the bay and at the mouth of the York River and were forced on some occasions to alter their schedules. The nation's railroads were also taxed to near capacity and there were major operational problems at many railroads. On December 26, 1917, President Woodrow Wilson signed a presidential order to nationalize the country's railroads and for the United States Railroad Administration

S. Davies Warfield was the Old Bay Line president who masterminded the first two sister ships in 1922 and 1923. He died before the third vessel was built so she was named *President Warfield* in his honor. (*Courtesy of The Enoch Pratt Free Library, Maryland's State Library Resource Center*)

January 1, 1921. It did so declaring that the dining room, galley, and accommodations "should be placed under the direct management of a woman experienced in the ways of housekeeping."[3] Mrs. Clotworthy had been head of the Red Cross's Canteen in Baltimore during World War I and was at that time proprietor of the Green Door Tea Room in Baltimore. She was to rise rapidly through the ranks of Old Bay Line management.

The company, meanwhile, continued with only the steamers *Florida* and *Alabama* with no backup vessel. At first the Bay Line considered the possibility of building a new superstructure on the *Virginia*'s steel hull, which, along with the machinery, had survived the fire in good order. However, in September 1919, Baltimore Dry Docks and Ship Building Company advised against such a move, saying it would be uneconomical. The same month, Bethlehem Steel presented the Bay Line with blueprints for a new steamer, but for unknown reasons, the line did not go ahead with building a new vessel.[4]

So that the *Alabama* could enter the shipyard to receive new boilers, the Old Bay Line turned to the Central Hudson Steamboat Company, which operated a fleet of steamers on the Hudson River, including the *Benjamin B. Odell*, which the Bay Line chartered for the winter of 1920–21. The *Odell* was a 280-foot four-deck steamer built in 1911 by Harlan & Hollingsworth. Once the *Alabama* rejoined the fleet and the *Odell* headed back north, the Old Bay Line still had only two passenger steamers.

The Chesapeake Line, meanwhile, decided to upgrade its vessels and in May 1922, when the *City of Baltimore* and *City of Norfolk* went into the shipyard for their spring overhaul, twenty-eight new staterooms and six additional bathrooms were built on the hurricane deck behind the wheelhouse and officers' quarters. At the same time, five additional bedrooms were added to the saloon deck. A little less than a year later, the *City of Atlanta* (ex-*Columbia*) spent ten weeks in the shipyard undergoing major interior and exterior renovations. Thirty additional staterooms, six additional baths, elevators for the loading and unloading of freight, and a refrigerating plant were among the renovations. In many ways, the Chesapeake Line was in better shape than the Old Bay Line, but that was about to change.

On February 2, 1922, S. Davies Warfield announced a major re-equipping of the Seaboard Air Line and the Baltimore Steam Packet Company. The plan called for the construction of many new freight cars to replace earlier ones that had become run down during federal operation, and twenty-five new locomotives. New passenger and freight vessels for the steamship company to be built by Pusey and Jones Corporation of Wilmington, Delaware, were also a major part of the plan. To facilitate this enormous project, a new corporation was formed on February 6 called the Seaboard-Bay Line Company to be headed by Warfield in Baltimore. To finance the plan, the new corporation negotiated a loan of $4.4 million from the U.S. government. The Interstate Commerce Commission approved the financing plan, setting in motion the massive construction program.[5]

The two new steamers were to be identical coal-burners measuring 330 feet long with a beam of 58 feet, powered by a single triple expansion engine of 3,800 indicated horsepower, giving them a design speed of 18.5 miles per hour. The vessels were converted to oil burning in the 1930s. The reciprocating engine had been in use on Old Bay Line steamers since the freighter *Gaston*, launched in 1881. The plans called for five decks, with the saloon and gallery decks devoted to staterooms and public rooms. An early artist's rendering shows the wheelhouse on the hurricane deck, three decks above the freight deck (like the Chesapeake liners of 1911) with only officers' quarters attached. The rest of the deck would have been open passenger space. Another later rendering showed passenger cabins and a covered deck area on the Hurricane Deck behind the wheelhouse and officers' quarters. There were to be 170 staterooms, a passenger capacity of 600, and a freight capacity of 700 tons. A large cargo cold storage area was to be located on the forward end of the lower deck and the vessels were to have a modern refrigeration plant and electric hoists for freight.[6]

They would be by far the largest steamers on the Chesapeake—nearly 30 feet longer than the *City of Norfolk* and *City of Baltimore*. The dining room, which on earlier Old Bay Line boats was located on the lower deck without any windows, was placed on the aft end of the main deck on the new ships, giving diners a panoramic view of the passing scenery through its many windows. It could seat 100 persons. The vessels' interior was in a Colonial style, and in addition to the usual lounges, a glass-enclosed palm room was located aft on the gallery deck where a live orchestra played for passengers dancing the evening away. There were also such amenities as a barber shop, shoe-shining service, clothes-pressing service, and telephones in each stateroom. They were described as "the most modern and best equipped in the inland waterways service out of Baltimore."[7] Whereas most bay steamers were wood from the main deck up, the twins were to have steel up to the saloon deck with the steel hull flared out to the main deck guards.

The keel of the first vessel, to be named *State of Maryland*, was laid on March 4, 1922. Her sister that soon followed was the *State of Virginia*. Construction moved quickly on both boats, and a large group of notables from Maryland and Virginia, including the mayor of Baltimore, traveled to Wilmington by special train for the launch of the *State of Maryland* on July 26, 1922. She was officially named by Mrs. C. Baker Clotworthy, by then superintendent of service for the Old Bay Line. The *State of Virginia*, which was taking shape nearby, was named on September 7, 1922, by Helen Sue Trinkle, the seven-year-old daughter of Virginia Governor E. Lee Trinkle.

The first of three modern sister ships built after World War I was the *State of Maryland,* which entered service in 1922. At 330 feet, she and her sisters were by far the largest steamers ever on the Bay. They had a passenger capacity of 531 and a cargo capacity of 82,526 cubic feet.

The *State of Maryland* was handed over to her new owners on November 30 and left Wilmington for Baltimore. Aboard were the distinguished naval architects William Francis Gibbs and Frederic Gibbs, who were paid $3,100 for their "inspection, advice, and supervision of the trial trip." Their report on the new steamer has unfortunately apparently been lost.[8] The Gibbs brothers later gained fame for designing the superliner *United States* after World War II.

Under the command of Captain William C. Almy, the company's senior master, the *State of Maryland* made her maiden voyage to Norfolk on the night of January 8, 1923, following an open house on board. The *State of Virginia*, commanded by Captain R. Sidney Foster, followed less than a month later, making her maiden voyage in early February 1923. The addition of identical modern steamers with a large freight capacity meant changes to the Bay Line fleet. The freighter *Gaston* was sold in 1920 and left the *Raleigh* as the company's only freighter. Once the new vessels had settled in, the company put the *Florida* on the market and opted to keep the *Alabama* of 1893 as its spare vessel. It is not clear why the *Alabama*, which was fifteen years older than the *Florida*, was retained rather than the newer ship. Perhaps it had something to do with her practically brand-new boilers. The *Florida* was sold to the Monticello Steamship Company of Vallejo, California, and ran for many years as a car ferry on San Francisco Bay.

For the next several years, the *State of Maryland* and *State of Virginia* held down the main passenger and freight service, being spelled from time to time by the *Alabama* when they were taken off line for inspection or regular maintenance. The *Alabama* was also used for charter operations several times during this period, but those occasions became fewer and farther apart by the mid-1920s. Mrs. Clotworthy, by then a vice president of the company,

Right: The new boats were decorated in colonial style—a marked departure from the Victorian styling of earlier bay steamers. This is the main staircase between the saloon and gallery decks.

Below: Looking aft on the spacious gallery deck on the *State of Virginia*, the second of the three sister ships. The doors to the staterooms that line the deck were mahogany. Note the stained-glass skylight in the overhead. (*Pusey and Jones Corp. photo, Accession #72.350 PO92-66, Hagley Museum and Library, Wilmington, Delaware*)

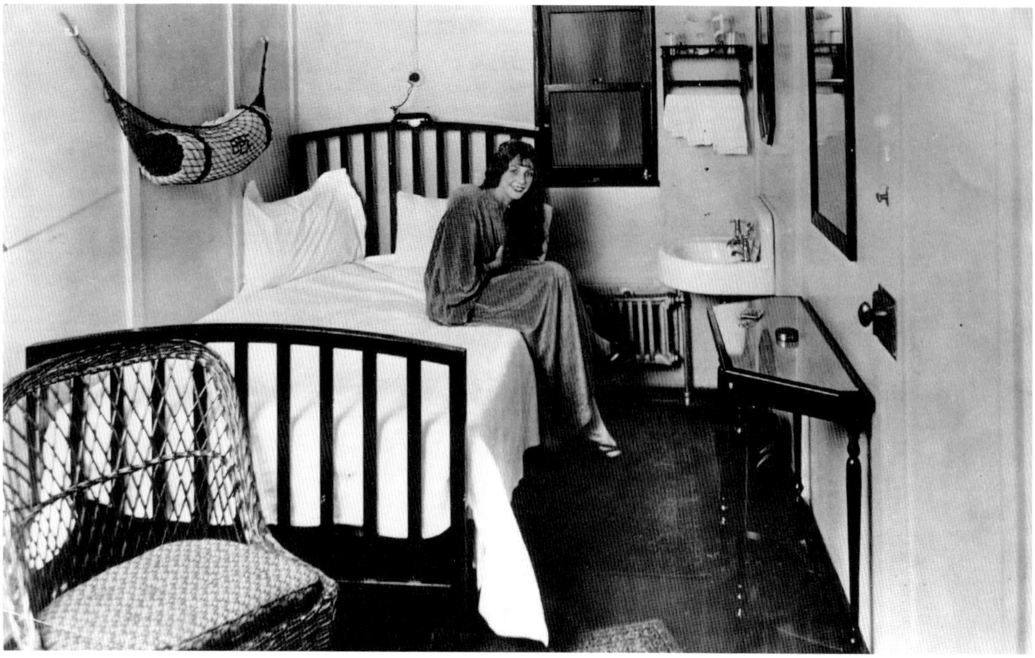

A bedroom on the *State of Maryland* provided all the amenities for an overnight voyage. The adjoining toilet and shower are off to one side out of the photo. (*Pusey and Jones Corp. photo Accession #72.350 PO Box 16 02-338, Courtesy of the Hagley Museum and Library, Wilmington, Delaware*)

Staterooms with upper and lower berths on the new vessels were roomier than their earlier counterparts and had space for two wicker chairs. (*Pusey and Jones Corp. photo Accession #72.360 PO-66, Courtesy of the Hagley Museum and Library, Wilmington, Delaware*)

The Old Bay Line created a wide variety of advertising materials to promote its sister ships. These two items are among the most colorful.

told President Warfield in a June 13, 1927, letter that efforts to charter the *Alabama* had been turned down several times with the business often going to the Chesapeake Line.[9]

Company officials began to think in terms of a third steamer built to the same plans as the *State of Maryland* and *State of Virginia*. Surprisingly, though, Warfield was not in favor of a third new boat, but Mrs. Clotworthy made a persuasive case for one. She wrote:

> The *Alabama*'s hull is very thin and a considerable number of plates will have to be renewed at her next dry docking at an approximate cost of $450 each; the electric wiring is obsolete and the entire boat should be rewired, in fact the whole boat and machinery should have a general overhauling … The cost would be in the neighborhood of $200,000 and then we would only have an old boat with none of the conveniences of our new ones.[10]

She went on to state that if a third steamer was built, one should not always be used simply as a spare, but that all three would rotate on the regular run, "giving each an annual four months rest, which would greatly lengthen the life of all the steamers," and mean a reduction in maintenance costs. That suggestion, however, was not adopted. Mrs. Clotworthy's proposal for a third steamer was taken up by the Old Bay Line board of directors, and apparently, she was very persuasive. At the conclusion of her presentation, Jacob Epstein, an influential board member, is reported to have simply turned to his colleagues and said, "Give the lady what she wants."[11]

A $959,970 contract was awarded to Pusey and Jones for a steamer to be an exact duplicate of the *State of Maryland*. Since most Bay Line passenger steamers were named for southern states, it was widely expected that the new boat would be named either *Florida* or *State of Florida*, but the record is not entirely clear on that detail. It would soon, however, be a moot point.

On October 24, 1927, S. Davies Warfield died suddenly at the age of sixty-four in a Baltimore hospital while recovering from an operation. He was widely mourned for his considerable impact in the world of business and finance. By sad coincidence, Key Compton, president of the Chesapeake Line, also died unexpectedly at the age of sixty-three several months earlier on May 5, 1927, and was succeeded by A. L. Stephens.[12]

Legh R. Powell, Jr., the Old Bay Line vice president who was in the hospital room with Warfield when he died, was elected president, and not long after, the board of directors voted to name the new steamer *President Warfield* in honor of the company's late leader. There was some controversy over the form of the name, wrote historian David C. Holly, who wrote that Mrs. Clotworthy felt that the name *President Warfield* seemed to suggest a ferryboat, and that the name should be *S. Davies Warfield*. That, however, was a battle she lost.[13] Later in her career, the vessel's name would cause occasional confusion when some reporters referred to her as the *President Garfield*, referring to the one-time president of the United States.

The new steamer was launched on February 6, 1928, in the presence of 500 invited guests. The naming honors went to Mrs. Zachary Lewis of Baltimore, Warfield's niece. It has been suggested that another of his nieces—Wallis Warfield Spencer—might have been sponsor had she not been in Europe where her first marriage was nearing an end. She married and divorced a second time in order to eventually marry the former King Edward VIII, who abdicated in order to marry her. They became known as the duke and duchess of Windsor.

In most ways, the *President Warfield* was identical to her earlier sister ships but had a larger than usual four-bladed solid manganese propeller and a German-designed high efficiency Oertz streamlined rudder that, along with the elimination of bilge keels, resulted in an increase in operating efficiency while steaming at high speed. That efficiency manifested itself during trials that began on July 12, 1928, from Wilmington to Baltimore by way of the offshore route along the Atlantic coast when she made 19.57 statute miles per hour, which was somewhat faster than her sister ships. She also required less horsepower than her sisters to maintain the contract top speed of 18.5 miles per hour.[14]

"This increase in speed at normal horsepower was aptly demonstrated when the *President Warfield*, leaving Old Point Comfort one half-hour after the *State of Virginia*, nevertheless docked next morning in Baltimore one hour ahead of the latter ship," reported *Marine Engineering and Shipping Age* in its September 1928 edition.[15]

Her maiden voyage took place from Baltimore to Norfolk on July 18, 1928. A commemorative menu was issued for that voyage that highlighted the Old Bay Line's famous cuisine. She was under the command of Captain William C. Almy. In its August 1928 edition, *The Nautical Gazette* referred to the *Warfield* as "modern in every respect" and "an addition of great value to the coastwise tonnage" of the port of Baltimore.[16] Another published report called the steamer "magnificent" and "the last word in inland water steamship construction."

Now that three new and modern steamers were in service, the Old Bay Line saw no need to retain the *Alabama* any longer. She was purchased by the Edmonds-Victoria Ferry Company of Seattle, Washington for use on a ferry run to Vancouver Island for many years. The addition of the *President Warfield* made the *State of Virginia* the spare boat. Now with three identical new steamers, the Old Bay Line had by far the finest and most modern fleet on Chesapeake Bay.

Above left: Having just been named by Warfield's niece, the *President Warfield* slides down the ways into the Cristiana River in Wilmington, Delaware, on February 6, 1928. She was the last steamer built for the Old Bay Line.

Above right: The Old Bay Line distributed this attractive booklet to attract passengers to its steamers in the 1930s when business was off due to the Depression.

The new sister ships had a covered promenade on the hurricane (or top) deck, which was a first for Bay Line steamers.

The handsome *President Warfield*—flagship of the company—coming into Baltimore harbor during the 1930s. The flag over the pilothouse indicates she is carrying U.S. Mail. (*Photo by Hans Marx*)

6

Depression Years, Prohibition, and Tragedy

With steamboats like those of the Old Bay Line and Chesapeake Line operating daily in the crowded harbors of Baltimore and Norfolk in all kinds of weather 365 days a year, there were bound to be accidents, especially when there was heavy fog. There were collisions involving the *City of Atlanta*, *City of Richmond*, *City of Norfolk*, and several other steamers during the twenties, all of which occurred in fog but were relatively minor. The most serious collision during this time, however, ended with the sinking of one of the finest steamers on the bay.

For fourteen years, the Chesapeake Line's *City of Richmond* and *City of Annapolis* ran virtually without incident on their Baltimore–West Point run, passing each other nightly in the vicinity of the Smith Point Lighthouse near the mouth of the Potomac River; but not on the night of February 24, 1927.

The *City of Annapolis* left West Point on schedule at 6 p.m. on February 23 bound for Baltimore with forty-seven passengers and thirty-three crew members. At the same time, the *City of Richmond* with thirty-six passengers and fifty-three crew departed Baltimore headed for York River landings. Shortly after midnight, heavy fog was encountered and the fog whistles of both steamers were sounded. Assistant Purser Harry Altman remembered the following years later:

> A few minutes later there was a jolting crash that threw us to the deck. I thought we had run into one of the schooners operating in the area. On deck, I saw at a glance that we had drifted into the path of the *Richmond*, which had rammed us on the port side.[1]

The *City of Richmond* cut deeply into the *Annapolis* before coming to a stop. Although there was a huge hole in the *Annapolis*'s hull and water surged in, the *Richmond* kept her propeller turning slowly so her bow would remain wedged in the opening. Had she not done so, the *Annapolis* might have sunk quickly.

With the two sister ships locked together, passengers on the *City of Annapolis* were rounded up by crew members and simply walked across the bow of the *City of Richmond*, which remained firmly wedged into the hole, helping keep her sister afloat. One person, a passenger killed in her cabin, was the only fatality.

Two other vessels had arrived on the scene to offer help—the tramp ship *St. Anthony* and the passenger steamer *Potomac* of the Baltimore and Virginia Steamboat Company. Once everyone had been safely transferred, the *Potomac* attempted to push the locked sisters into shallow water, but it was too late.

As the *City of Annapolis* settled lower with the *Richmond*'s bow still embedded in her side, she was pulling her sister down, and at one point, the propeller and rudder of the *City of Richmond* were well above the water. Then the ships broke free of one another and the *Richmond*, which was not in any danger of sinking, backed off while her sister ship slowly sank bow first into 72 feet of water.[2] She had remained afloat about an hour and fifteen minutes after the collision.

The Chesapeake Line initially considered raising the *City of Annapolis* but a diver who examined the wreck a few days later described it as badly broken up with the funnel and wheelhouse both gone. As it now had only the *City of Richmond* and *City of Atlanta* on the York River run with no backup vessel, the Chesapeake Line quickly ordered a new ship from the Newport News Shipbuilding and Drydock Company. The new steamer, named *Yorktown*, was nearly identical to the *City of Richmond*, with only minor differences in appearance. She was launched in February 1928, a little more than two weeks after the Old Bay Line's *President Warfield*, making her the last overnight steamer to be built for Chesapeake Bay service.

By this time, Prohibition was in full swing and there was widespread bootlegging. The steamers of the Old Bay Line and Chesapeake Line soon found themselves unwittingly caught up in the net of bootlegging.

The *City of Baltimore* and *City of Norfolk* were boarded in Norfolk in January 1927 by federal officials who had been tipped off that both steamers had illegal liquor aboard. Five people were arrested and a substantial amount of whiskey was recovered on board the vessel. The *State of Maryland* was boarded at Old Point Comfort on March 4 and federal officials turned up 6 gallons of liquor concealed in the crew's quarters, but no arrests were made. Then things heated up a bit.

On the night of March 4, 1929, the *President Warfield* was more than halfway through her nightly run down the bay below Wolf Trap Light when two Coast Guard patrol boats pulled near, sounded their sirens, and ordered her to stop. When she did not, the patrol boats fired two blank shots across her bow and then a solid shot. It was still dark at the time, and First Officer John L. Marshall, who was on watch, said he never heard the sirens and there is no indication that a searchlight was used. Captain William C. Almy ordered the vessel stopped to determine what was going on. Coast Guard officers said they had been tipped off to the presence of illegal alcoholic beverages aboard and they were proven right when 129 gallons of liquor was discovered in a car on the freight deck and in the rooms of some engine room personnel.[3] The smugglers were never found, but the incident ignited a brief controversy.

Captain Almy filed a protest and shipping interests in the area expressed their displeasure over the firing on the steamer. Maryland Senator Millard Tydings wrote Coast Guard Rear Admiral Frederick Billard asking for a thorough investigation. He felt the vessel should have been searched before departure or when she arrived in Norfolk. A Coast Guard official in Norfolk said the original plan was to search the *Warfield* when she got to Old Point Comfort, but word of that plan leaked out and it was decided to board the steamer before she docked to prevent the car in question from getting ashore with

The *City of Richmond* in a Baltimore ship repair yard after ramming and sinking her sister ship *City of Annapolis* in heavy fog on February 24, 1927. The *Annapolis* was a total loss. (*Courtesy of Ted Baldwin*)

The Chesapeake Line quickly ordered a new steamer to replace the *City of Annapolis*. She was named the *Yorktown* and was virtually identical to the lost steamer. Launched in February 1928 in Newport News, Virginia, she was the last night boat built for service on Chesapeake Bay. (*Courtesy of Huntington Ingalls Industries*)

its contraband. Admiral Billard soon decreed that no longer would passenger steamers be halted on the open bay, calling such stops unnecessary. Although bay steamers would continue to be searched when in port, none was ever again ordered to stop while *en route*.

There were more and more automobiles and trucks using improved roads in the bay region in the 1920s, and over time, they took some business away from the steamboats. The Old Bay Line and Chesapeake Line eventually found it expedient to carry passengers' cars on the freight deck while their owners relaxed, dined, and slept several decks above. That way, as soon as the steamer docked, passengers could drive right off the pier refreshed and continue on their way. The companies emphasized that motorists saved 230 miles of driving that way. Initially, gasoline was drained from the cars as a safety measure, but in time, that practice ended. During the period between the world wars, a passenger could bring a car along for as little as $4. It was only $8 in 1961.[4]

The year 1932 saw the end of an era for the Old Bay Line when Captain Almy retired after sixty-one years at sea, forty-four of them with the Old Bay Line. His first command for the Bay Line was the *Carolina* when she came out in 1877. He was said to have entertained presidents Taft, Wilson, and Theodore Roosevelt at his table. Captain R. Sydney Foster became senior master following Almy's retirement. Almy died in 1939.

The Great Depression had a considerable impact on all Chesapeake Bay steamboat lines. Business dropped off so much that when a wharf needed rebuilding such as after a bad storm, or a steamer required updated equipment, many lines could not afford it and went out of business. Far fewer people were traveling, and in the case of the steamers of the Old Bay Line and Chesapeake Line, two large boats were sailing each night in each direction more empty than full leading to significant losses of revenue and operating losses during those lean years.

With its three practically brand-new steamers, the Bay Line was in better condition than the Chesapeake Line, but both were hurting. Although the railroad owners of the Chesapeake Line—the Southern Railway and Atlantic Coast Line—ideally wanted to continue to have a steamship line entry into Baltimore, it was readily apparent that there was a declining need for two steamship lines and that led to the start of negotiations in 1937 that later ultimately resulted in the merger of the two lines.

Rather than having its spare steamer tied up and going nowhere during these lean periods, the Old Bay Line chartered the *State of Virginia* several times during the 1930s to the Colonial Navigation Company, which operated an overnight line on Long Island Sound. The *President Warfield* was also chartered to Colonial and Eastern Steamship Lines for entire summers on several occasions during the same period. The income from the charters was welcomed by the company's financial people. The *State of Virginia* also ran a number of charter trips on the Chesapeake for private organizations, political parties, businesses, religious groups, and others. In June 1934, for instance, she carried members of church and patriotic groups to St. Mary's City, Maryland, as part of the 300th anniversary of the founding of Maryland. A Roman Catholic mass was celebrated aboard the ship as she sailed past St. Clement's Island, where the first Roman Catholic mass in English North America was celebrated in 1634.

On July 15, 1936 during one of these cruises, she was carrying 235 delegates of the Automobile Trade Association on a convention cruise when she was rammed on the port side by the freighter *Golden Harvest* near the mouth of the Patapsco River. Among the passengers was Maryland Governor Harry W. Nice, but neither he nor anyone else

Above left: The Old Bay Line began carrying passengers' cars aboard its steamers in the late 1920s—a practice that proved extremely popular and lucrative.

Above right: After the captain, the purser was arguably the most important man on board. He was essentially the vessel's hotel manager. Harry C. Baker was purser for many years on the *President Warfield*. (*Courtesy of Donna O'Neill*)

On a number of occasions in the twentieth century, the Chesapeake Bay froze over during particularly cold winters. This is 1918 and the *Virginia* or *Florida* is tied up in Norfolk harbor, which is completely covered by ice. No vessels at all moved for close to thirty days because of the ice.

Above: The *City of Norfolk* pushes through heavy ice near the mouth of the Magothy River in 1934. The steamers rarely got stuck in heavy ice.

Left: While serving as a backup steamer for the regular Baltimore–Norfolk boats in the 1930s, the *State of Virginia* was often chartered by various groups for special cruises. Here she is pulling out of Pier Ten, Light Street, on one such charter.

on either vessel was injured. At no time was the *State of Virginia* in danger of sinking. The two vessels stayed locked together while passengers transferred to the Love Point ferry *Pittsburgh*, which took them to Baltimore.

Starting in 1936 and lasting through 1940, the *State of Virginia* became a cruise ship and operated a number of summertime houseboat cruises, in which passengers used the ship as a hotel over several days while visiting different ports in Virginia. The publicity department vigorously promoted the cruises with such purple prose as "a thrillingly different vacation," "joyous, blithesome hours of moonlight," daytime cruising on the "sun-kissed waters of the bay," and "it is surprising how much sheer joy can be crowded into three nights and two days."[5]

Those weekend trips began in Baltimore on Friday evenings with an overnight trip down the bay to an offshore cruise along the Virginia coast Saturday morning. The vessel then anchored for the rest of Saturday off Ocean View, Virginia, near the mouth of the bay, where passengers could change into swimsuits in their staterooms and then be ferried to the beach for swimming. In the evening, there was a beach bonfire with what else—hot dogs cooked over an open fire. For those so inclined, they could remain on the steamer and fish right from her decks at the anchorage. The lucky fishermen turned their catches over to the chef for their evening meal.

Early Sunday morning, she departed for Yorktown where passengers could visit the historic colonial town itself, or nearby Williamsburg, or Jamestown. That afternoon, the steamer departed for Norfolk for sightseeing before leaving at 6:30 p.m. for Baltimore, arriving on Monday morning. On the way, there was dancing to a live orchestra in the palm room to round out the cruise. The cost of the cruises ranged from $15.50 to $24 and included transportation, stateroom, eight meals aboard ship, and trips ashore.

During the summer of 1941, the itinerary was altered somewhat, and the Ocean View visit was replaced with swimming and a hot dog roast on the beach while at Yorktown. The option of a daylight cruise of the James River was also added for those passengers who did not tour the historic sites. It turned out that 1941 was the last season for the houseboat cruises.

Both steamboat lines also offered less ambitious all-expense weekend travel packages on a regular basis in the 1930s between Baltimore and Norfolk that included a one-night stay at a fine Norfolk or Virginia Beach hotel.

In 1937, the first of several labor issues that would eventually have a lasting effect on the company came to the fore. With no advance warning, a labor union official confronted company Vice President Robert E. Dunn in April and told him that a strike would be called that evening over inadequate working conditions and inadequate pay. Although a temporary accommodation was quickly reached through negotiation, several crew members on the *State of Maryland* and *President Warfield* walked off their jobs that same evening, delaying the departure of both boats and inconveniencing a large number of passengers. Ultimately, however, following negotiations between the two sides, a vote was held, and Bay Line employees rejected union representation.

A major disaster struck on the evening of July 29, 1937, when the Chesapeake Line's *City of Baltimore*, with 150 people aboard, caught fire outside of Baltimore harbor while bound for Norfolk. The fire apparently began on the freight deck and spread rapidly through the steamer's wooden superstructure. Captain Charles O. Brooks later said that within three minutes, the ship was ablaze from stem to stern.[6] The heat

For a number of years in the 1930s and early 1940s, the *State of Virginia* ran what were called "Houseboat Cruises" in which passengers used the boat as their hotel while the steamer visited a number of historic sites in the lower bay over the course of several days.

The twentieth century steamers of the Old Bay Line had triple-expansion reciprocating engines that provided their power. Here the chief engineer observes as an engine room crew member operates equipment aboard the *Provincetown* (previously the *District of Columbia*). (*Photo by Conrad Milster*)

This is the boiler room of the *City of Norfolk* looking forward. She had four boilers, two to each side of the boiler room. When built, she was coal-fired, but was converted to oil burning in 1944. (*Photo by Conrad Milster*)

The *City of Richmond*'s Chief Engineer Donald Whitlock stands next to the engine room telegraph where commands from the wheelhouse were received and acknowledged. (*Photo by Hans Marx*)

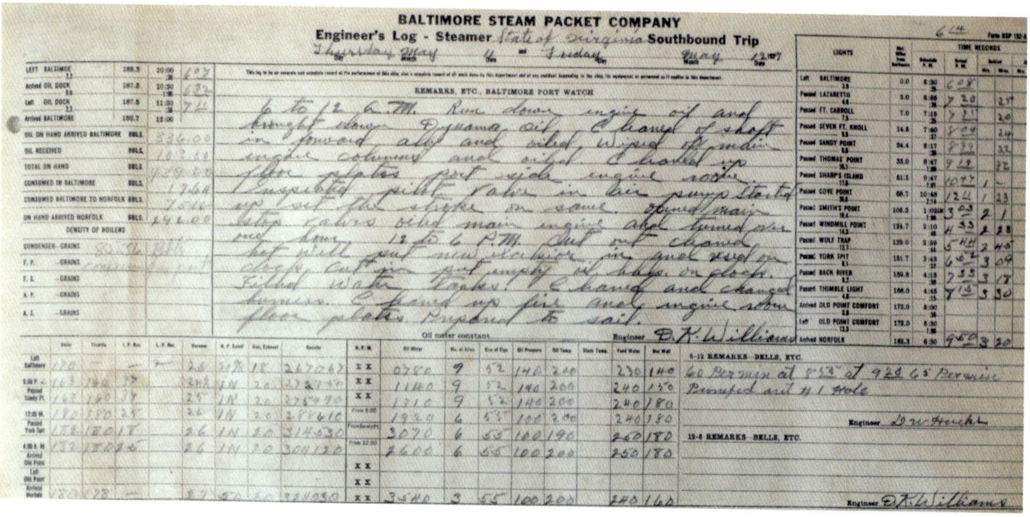

BALTIMORE STEAM PACKET COMPANY

Engineer's Log - Steamer State of Virginia Southbound Trip

Thursday May 11 and Friday May 12 197

REMARKS, ETC., BALTIMORE PORT WATCH

6 to 12 A.M. Run down engine oil and brought down Dynamo oil. Cleaned of shaft in forward alley and oiled. Wiped off main engine columns and oiled. Cleaned up floor plates port side engine room. Inspected pilot valve in air pump. Started up set the stroke on same. Opened main stop valves oiled main engine and turned over one hour. 12 to 6 P.M. Cut out cleaned hot well put new washer in and used on deck. Cut in put empty oil bbls. on deck. Filled water tanks. Cleaned and changed burners. Cleaned up fire and engine room floor plates. Prepared to sail.

Engineer D. K. Williams

6-12 REMARKS—BELLS, ETC.

60 Per min at 8:53 at 9:23 65 Per min

Pumped out #1 Hold

Engineer D. W. Knight

12-6 REMARKS—BELLS, ETC.

Engineer D. K. Williams

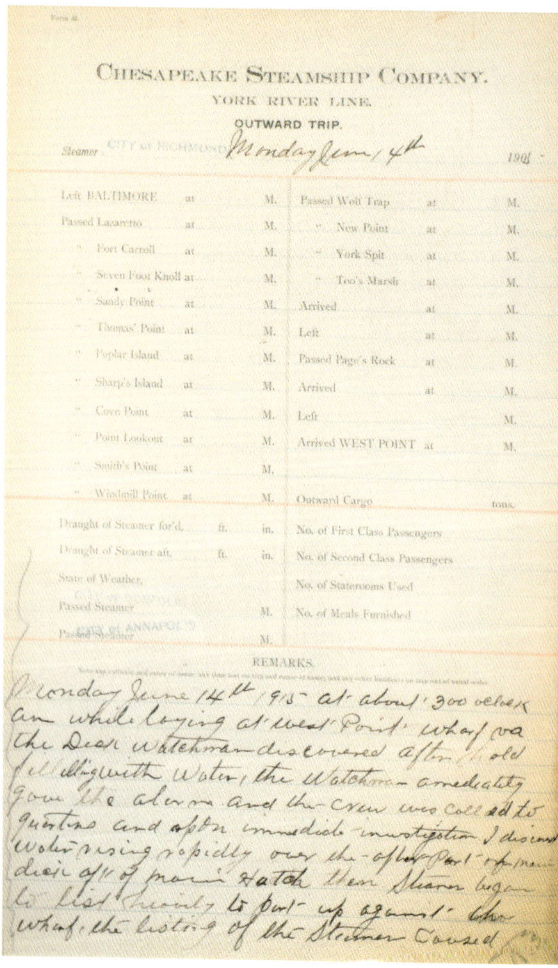

CHESAPEAKE STEAMSHIP COMPANY.

YORK RIVER LINE.

OUTWARD TRIP.

Steamer CITY OF RICHMOND Monday June 14th 1915

Left BALTIMORE	at	M.	Passed Wolf Trap	at	M.
Passed Lazaretto	at	M.	" New Point	at	M.
" Fort Carroll	at	M.	" York Spit	at	M.
" Seven Foot Knoll	at	M.	" Too's Marsh	at	M.
" Sandy Point	at	M.	Arrived	at	M.
" Thomas' Point	at	M.	Left	at	M.
" Poplar Island	at	M.	Passed Page's Rock	at	M.
" Sharp's Island	at	M.	Arrived	at	M.
" Cove Point	at	M.	Left		M.
" Point Lookout	at	M.	Arrived WEST POINT	at	M.
" Smith's Point	at	M.			
" Windmill Point	at	M.	Outward Cargo		tons.
Draught of Steamer for'd.	ft.	in.	No. of First Class Passengers		
Draught of Steamer aft.	ft.	in.	No. of Second Class Passengers		
State of Weather.			No. of Staterooms Used		
Passed Steamer CITY OF NORFOLK		M.	No. of Meals Furnished		
Passed Steamer CITY OF ANNAPOLIS		M.			

REMARKS.

Monday June 14th 1915 at about 3 00 oclock am while laying at West Point wharf va the Deck Watchman discovered after hold filling with water, the Watchman immediately gave the alarm and the crew was called to quarters and after immediate investigation I discovered water rising rapidly over the after part of main deck aft of main Hatch then Steamer began to list heavily to port up against the wharf. the listing of the Steamer caused

Above: Engineers on the steamers kept a detailed log of their many activities, which included operating, maintaining, and repairing the ship's engines and all the other machinery required to keep a large steam-powered vessel going. (*The Estate of Hans Marx*)

Left: Detailed logs were maintained in the steamers' pilothouses, noting weather, navigational aids, other vessels, landmarks passed, and unusual events. This log page from the *City of Richmond* when she was with the Chesapeake Line includes the entry recording her 1915 sinking. Old Bay Line logs were very similar. (*Courtesy of the Collection of Hans Marx*)

forced many passengers to jump overboard to be rescued by a number of vessels that quickly arrived on the scene. Among the rescue vessels was the Old Bay Line's *State of Maryland.* Brooks said later that several lifeboats succeeded in getting away from the burning vessel as she drifted aground on a shoal near Bodkin Point.

By midnight, all that was left of the *City of Baltimore* was her steel hull, funnel, and ventilators poking out through the smoking debris that had been her superstructure. Four people died in the conflagration, including two passengers. In the immediate aftermath of the fire, there were suggestions that it may have been set deliberately. Captain Brooks said he could think of no other reason for the fire to have spread so rapidly, but federal investigators soon ruled out the sabotage theory. One of the investigators said he believed a cigar or cigarette had been smoldering among the freight since before the ship left the dock, but no cause was ever determined.

Following the fire, the Chesapeake Line took the *Yorktown* off the York River run and diverted her to take the *City of Baltimore*'s place on the Norfolk line with the *City of Norfolk.* That left the *City of Richmond* to handle the York River route on an every-other-day basis. The fire, however, had far-reaching implications. New safety at sea regulations took effect on October 1, 1937, and were strictly enforced. For the Chesapeake Line, that meant that its three remaining steamers could not carry passengers until automatic sprinkler systems were installed. They carried freight only until the work was completed. The *City of Richmond* was the first of the fleet to be equipped and returned to service in the middle of October. The *City of Norfolk* and *Yorktown* followed soon after. The Old Bay Line steamers had their sprinkler systems installed at the same time. Unfortunately, a casualty of the new fire regulations was the Western Shore Steamboat Company, sole survivor of the bay's once-flourishing river steamer fleet. It folded because it could not afford a sprinkler system.

As the 1930s drew to a close, the vessels of the Old Bay Line and Chesapeake Line continued their nightly voyages on the Chesapeake Bay and York River largely without incident. However, big changes were looming just over the horizon.

On July 29, 1937, the *City of Baltimore* caught fire outside of Baltimore harbor and was destroyed. All that was left was the steel hull and steel engine and boiler casings. Four people lost their lives in the disaster.

7

Cuisine on the Bay

Passengers embarking on the night boats between Baltimore and Norfolk had more than just a pleasant voyage awaiting them. One of the chief attractions of traveling overnight on the Chesapeake Bay was the cuisine offered in the vessels' dining rooms—dinner in the evening and breakfast in the morning, always with an emphasis on local fare.

When the Old Bay Line was founded, steamers departed at 4 p.m. and arrived at the other end of the bay around 6 or 6:30 the next morning—plenty of time in which to enjoy the pleasantries of the galley. In his centennial history of the company, Alexander Crosby Brown wrote of a typical voyage from Baltimore to Norfolk in 1840 and touched upon the dining experience of the day. Noting that the dining room was on a lower deck without windows or portholes, "the meal was a cheerful one with white napery and silver glistening in the light cast by whale-oil tapers."[1]

Dining rooms on Chesapeake Bay steamers were most often located toward the stern below the freight deck and had no windows. It was not until the first decade of the twentieth century that they were moved higher in certain vessels, giving diners a view of the passing scenery while they ate. On some boats, there were no permanent dining rooms, and in such cases chairs and tables were set up in one of the saloons for meals and then were taken down once the meal was ended. Over the decades, the Chesapeake Bay steamboat lines employed chefs who brought to the boats a wide variety of cooking knowledge with a decidedly Southern leaning. The waiters were dignified men with an approach to service that rivalled, or exceeded, anything that could be found in the finest hotels and restaurants ashore.

As the steamers grew larger and improved over the years, so did the on-board dining experience. By the 1890s, which is considered by most historians to have been the pinnacle of steamer travel on the Bay, the Old Bay Line was making quite a name for itself with its meals. Its $1 *à la carte* dinner was justly famous for its fare—Mobjack Bay oysters, diamondback terrapin, canvasback duck, quail, Norfolk spot, turkey, beefsteak, and the ever-popular Maryland fried chicken.

With the departure time at 6:30 p.m., the serving of the evening meal began shortly after sailing, giving passengers until 9 p.m. to enjoy their meals at a leisurely pace. In the morning, they could remain on board well after the 6:30 a.m. arrival time in order to enjoy the hearty breakfasts for which the South was so famous.

Above: Dining rooms on most steamers, like this one on the *Alabama*, were located aft on the lower deck, which meant there were no windows because they were below the waterline.

Right: Fine food was always a major drawing card for the Old Bay Line. This menu from 1884 gives an idea of the various breakfast dishes of the time.

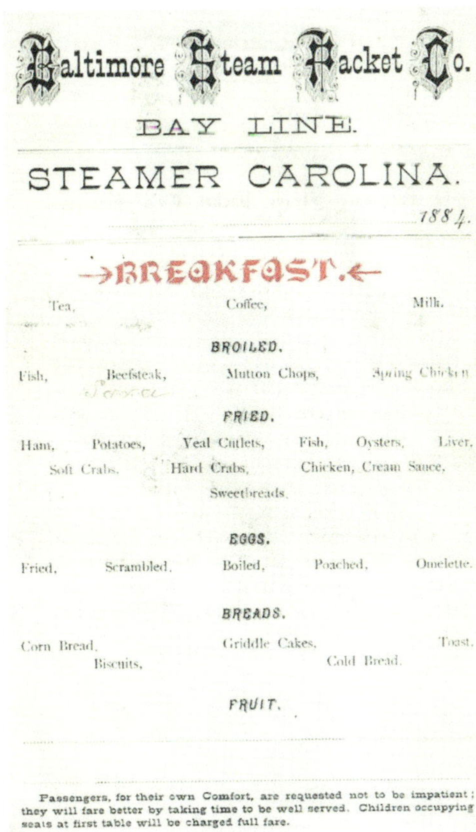

Baltimore Steam Packet Co.

BAY LINE.

STEAMER CAROLINA.

1884.

→BREAKFAST.←

Tea, Coffee, Milk.

BROILED.

Fish, Beefsteak, Mutton Chops, Spring Chicken

FRIED.

Ham, Potatoes, Veal Cutlets, Fish, Oysters, Liver,
Soft Crabs, Hard Crabs, Chicken, Cream Sauce,
Sweetbreads.

EGGS.

Fried, Scrambled, Boiled, Poached, Omelette.

BREADS.

Corn Bread, Griddle Cakes, Toast,
Biscuits, Cold Bread.

FRUIT.

Passengers, for their own Comfort, are requested not to be impatient; they will fare better by taking time to be well served. Children occupying seats at first table will be charged full fare.

BALTIMORE STEAM PACKET COMPANY
[OLD BAY LINE]

A LA CARTE
DINNER

Relishes
Fruit Cocktail 30 Queen Olives 20 Mixed Pickles 20 Hearts of Celery 20 Spiced Melon Rind 20
Tomato Juice Cocktail 20

Sea Food
Little Neck Clam on Half Shell 30 Cocktail 35 Grilled Salmon Trout 50
Shad Roe with Bacon 75 Crab Flake Cocktail 40

Soups
Consommé 25 Cream of Tomato 25 Mock Turtle 25 Crab Gumbo, Creole 25

Grilled, Etc.
Lamb Chops, each 35 Extra Sirloin Steak 1.25 Filet Mignon 80 Broiled Ham 60
Broiled Bacon 50 Bacon with Eggs 55 Ham with Eggs 55 Fricassee of Chicken 75

Vegetables
Potatoes
Lyonnaise
Hashed, Browned,
French Fried, Steamed or
Mashed 25
Potatoes au Gratin 30
Green Peas 25
New Asparagus 35
Corn in Cream 25
String Beans 25
Fried Egg Plant 35

Sandwiches
Tongue 25
Ham 20 Chicken 30
Club 65 Egg 20
Ham and Egg 30
Cheese 20

Bread, Etc.
Assorted Bread 10
Hot Rolls 10
Dry or Buttered Toast 15
Cream Toast 35
Milk Toast 25
Bran Muffins 10
Corn Cakes with
Maple Syrup 30

TABLE D'HOTE DINNER

FRUIT COCKTAIL WITH SHERRY
LITTLE NECK CLAM COCKTAIL
STUFFED CELERY RIPE OLIVES
CRAB GUMBO, CREOLE CONSOMMÉ PRINTANIÈRE

SHAD ROE WITH BACON
GRILLED SALMON TROUT WITH CORN CAKES
FRICASSEE OF CHICKEN, PARISIENNE
FILET MIGNON BORDELAISE
NEW POTATOES FRIED EGG PLANT
NEW ASPARAGUS, DRAWN BUTTER

ENDIVE AND AVOCADO SALAD

CARAMEL PIE, MERINGUE
FRESH STRAWBERRY SUNDAE CAKE
CREAMED CHEESE WITH GUAVA JELLY,
TOASTED CRACKERS

COFFEE TEA MILK
SANKA KAFFEE HAG

MEALS $1.25

[SMOKING PERMITTED]

Cold Meats, Salads, Etc.
Cold Sliced Chicken 65
Ham 50
with Potato Salad 60
Head Lettuce 35
Lettuce and
Tomato Salad 35
Lettuce and
Pineapple Salad 35
Chicken Salad 75
Potato Salad 30
Fruit Salad 35
Endive & Avocado Salad 35
(Choice of French, Mayonnaise or Thousand Island Dressing with Salads.)

Fruits, Desserts, Etc.
Sliced Pineapple 25
Preserved Figs
with Cream 30
Prunes with Cream 25
Extracted Honey 25
Ice Cream 20
Sundae 25
Assorted Cake 15
Caramel Pie 20
Florida Grapefruit 15
Cream Cheese with
Guava Jelly 25

Cheese with Crackers
American 25 Imported Roquefort 30 Swiss Gruyère 30

Beverages
Coffee, Cup 15, Pot for One 20 Tea, Pot 20 Cocoa, Pot 20 Milk, Individual Bottle 15
Postum, Kaffee Hag or Sanka 20 Canada Dry Ginger Ale 25 Cosman's Ginger Ale 20 Appolinaris Water 35
White Rock 30 Poland Water, Qts. 40 Budweiser 25 Arrow Special 20

Cigars Imported 25 and 35, Clear Havana and Domestic 15, 2 for 25 and 10 Cigarettes—All standard brands

Guests will please write orders on checks furnished by the Steward and pay only the total indicated thereon. Suggestions for the betterment of the service are solicited. C. E. Bell, *Superintendent Dining Service*, Baltimore, Md.

A typical dinner menu from the 1930s and 1940s shows that there were many dishes from which to choose.

A Chesapeake Line dinner menu from June 1900 began with oysters prepared in a variety of ways—fried, escalloped, broiled, stewed, and pâtés. They were followed by several cold meats, including ham, tongue, and corned beef, which led to hot meats such as chicken, beefsteak, and chops. There were seven items to select from under the choices of fried food, including pig's feet. A variety of relishes, breads, and fruits rounded out the selections. Beaufont Lithia Water—said to be one of the purest waters known—was on every table. As on most passenger trains, diners were asked to check off on a form the items they wanted from the menu—waiters did not write down any orders. The cost for a dinner on a steamer in June 1900 was 75 cents. "A little time is required for cooking. Passengers, for their own comfort, are requested not to be impatient; they will fare better by taking time to be well served," the notice at the bottom of the menu stated.[2]

The number of passengers who could be served at any one time varied from vessel to vessel. The *City of Baltimore* and *City of Norfolk*, with their dining rooms located on the forward end of the gallery deck, could seat sixty-two diners at a time. The *State of Maryland* class of steamers of 1923–28 of the Old Bay Line could seat 100 passengers at a time in their dining rooms located aft on the main deck.

Immaculate white linen tablecloths and napkins, along with silver flatware and hollow ware, created specifically for each line added to the air of elegance in the dining rooms. Those items are highly prized today by collectors.

Dinner menus became even more varied as the years went by and both lines offered meals *à la carte* or *Table d'Hote*, the latter costing $1.25 during the first decades of the twentieth century. At times, the Old Bay Line would also offer a "Bay Line Special" for 85 cents with a choice of three entrees, soups, and vegetables. Diners could choose from

When the *State of Maryland* and her sisters were built in the 1920s, the handsome dining room was placed aft on the main deck, providing diners with fresh air and views of the outdoors.

These are just a few examples of the many different types of china that were used on the Old Bay Line ships. The large pitcher is the only item not used in the dining room. It was used for drinking water in staterooms.

a number of dishes created from the bounty of the Chesapeake Bay and the surrounding country. Oysters, fish, and crabs were almost always on the menu, accompanied by an old Maryland and Virginia favorite—corn cakes. Fried chicken á la Maryland was a long-standing favorite as was the signature Virginia dish of Smithfield ham.

As sumptuous as dinner was, breakfast was no small affair either. An undated menu offered three club breakfasts for 50, 60, or 75 cents that included a variety of dishes such as eggs, corn cakes with maple syrup, bacon, ham, rolls, fruit, and coffee. On the *à la carte* breakfast menu were no fewer than nine varieties of eggs, six varieties of meats, four different types of potatoes, fish, eleven kinds of juices and jams, and an assortment of breads.

An Old Bay Line breakfast menu from the 1950s offered both a club breakfast for $1 or *à la carte* service. Broiled salt mackerel, local sausage links, corned beef hash with poached eggs, fried tomato slices with bacon, eggs, griddle cakes, cereals, and juices and coffee were to be found on the club breakfast menu. The *à la carte* offerings were fewer in number but still provided a lot of variety.

In the 1930s, following the repeal of Prohibition, both lines provided passengers with extensive beverage lists including as many as twelve different wines, cocktails with names like "Clover Club" and "Orange Blossom," cordials and liqueurs, fourteen liquors with such local favorites as mint juleps and five-year-old rye for which Maryland was famous. There were ten brands of beer—with well-known local names like American, Gunther, Baltimore Brew, Free State, and National. There were also soft drinks and other non-alcoholic beverages. Liquors and cocktails were served in the dining room, palm room on the *Warfield* class steamers, the social hall, and in staterooms.

Whenever the steamers deviated from their usual routine to operate charters or the weekend houseboat cruises offered in the 1930s, special menus were provided. In such cases luncheon was also served, bringing to the table such dishes as chicken á la king, imperial deviled crab, and panned Norfolk Spot. Of course, on the evening of May 23, 1940 there was a most special menu—a dinner on the *President Warfield* commemorating the Old Bay Line's centennial anniversary. It featured terrapin *à la Chesapeake*, roast golden pheasant, centennial salad, and a different wine or liqueur for each course. "An Old Bay Line meal is synonymous of gustatory titillation," the anniversary menu stated with a flourish.[3]

Recent research has uncovered information suggesting that at least some of the menus and recipes for meals on the Old Bay Line may have originated with parent company Seaboard Air Line Railway. A 1932 letter to Old Bay Line Purchasing Agent G. W. Schuncke from the Seaboard's superintendent of dining cars (whose signature is illegible) discusses new dinner menus and where to purchase the best ingredients for use in the preparation of various dishes. Enclosed with the letter was a recipe for a caramel meringue pie.

The Old Bay Line maintained the same high standard of dining service up to the very last day of passenger operations in the fall of 1961. The linen tablecloths and napkins had disappeared as an economy move by then but the food remained excellent to the end. The last menu may not have been as extensive as those at the turn of the twentieth century, but there were still old favorites such as Southern fried chicken, broiled fish, Maryland crab cakes, and filet mignon.

Those who had the privilege of dining on the Norfolk steamers long remembered those culinary delights.

BALTIMORE STEAM PACKET COMPANY
(OLD BAY LINE)

BREAKFAST A LA CARTE

FRUITS, Etc.
Strawberries with Cream 25 Stewed Rhubarb 20 Florida Grapefruit, half 15
Oranges, each 15 Sliced 20 Juice 20 Prunes with Cream 25 Preserved Figs 30
Florida Orange Marmalade 25 Extracted Honey 25 Tomato Juice Cocktail 20

CEREAL WITH CREAM
Rice Flakes 25 Corn Flakes 25 Shredded Wheat Biscuit 25 Bran Flakes 25
Steamed Oatmeal 25 Grape Nuts 25

FISH, Etc.
Broiled or Fried Fresh Fish 50

GRILLED, Etc.
Ham 50; Half Portion 25 Bacon 50; Half Portion 25 Lamb Chops, each 35
Breakfast Steak 80 Ham and Eggs 55 Bacon and Eggs 55
Minced Ham with Scrambled Eggs 65

EGGS
Boiled, Fried or Scrambled 25 Poached on Toast 35 Plain Omlet 35
Ham, Bacon or Fruit Omlet 50, Spanish 65

POTATOES
Hashed and Browned 20 French Fried 20 Hashed in Cream 20

BREAD
Hot Rolls 10 Corn Muffins 10 Dry or Buttered Toast 15 Milk Toast 25
Cream Toast 35 Griddle Cakes with Maple Syrup 30

BEVERAGES
Coffee, Cup 15; Pot for One 20 Tea, Pot 20 Cocoa, Pot 20 Milk, Individual Bottle 15
Postum, Kaffee Hag or Sanka 20

CLUB BREAKFAST MENU

No. 1—50c
Choice of Fruit or Cereal
Hot Rolls Toast Corn Muffins
Griddle Cakes with Maple Syrup
Eggs as Desired
Coffee Tea Cocoa Milk
Kaffee Hag Sanka

No. 2—60c
Choice of Fruit or Cereal
Hot Rolls Toast Corn Muffins
Griddle Cakes with Maple Syrup
Eggs Any Style with Bacon or Ham
Coffee Tea Cocoa Milk
Kaffee Hag Sanka

No. 3—75c
Choice of Fruit Choice of Cereal
Shad Roe with Bacon
Broiled or Fried Fresh Fish
Broiled Lamb Chops
Ham or Bacon with Eggs
Hot Rolls Toast Corn Muffins
Griddle Cakes with Maple Syrup
Coffee Tea Cocoa Milk
Kaffee Hag Sanka

Guests will please write orders on checks furnished by the Steward and pay only the total indicated thereon. Suggestions for the betterment of the service are solicited.

C. E. BELL, *Superintendent Dining Service,*
Baltimore, Md.

[SMOKING PERMITTED]

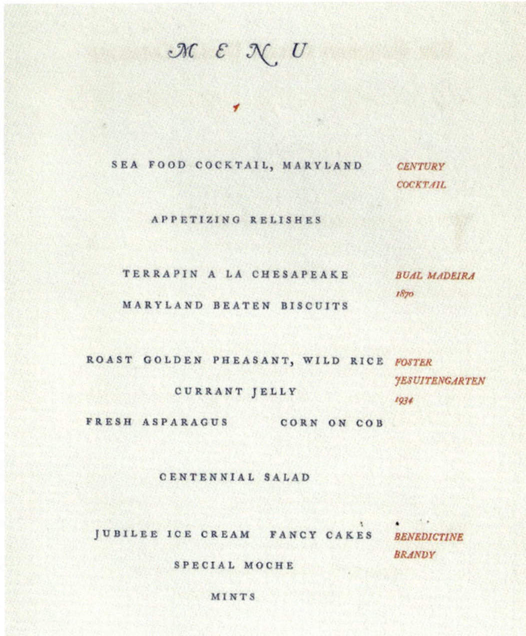

MENU

SEA FOOD COCKTAIL, MARYLAND — CENTURY COCKTAIL

APPETIZING RELISHES

TERRAPIN A LA CHESAPEAKE — BUAL MADEIRA 1870
MARYLAND BEATEN BISCUITS

ROAST GOLDEN PHEASANT, WILD RICE — FOSTER JESUITENGARTEN 1934
CURRANT JELLY
FRESH ASPARAGUS CORN ON COB

CENTENNIAL SALAD

JUBILEE ICE CREAM FANCY CAKES — BENEDICTINE BRANDY
SPECIAL MOCHE
MINTS

Above left: There was a lot of variety in this 1930s breakfast menu as well as several serving options from which to select.

Above right: The menu for the centennial dinner served aboard the *President Warfield* on May 23, 1940.

Below: Each piece of silver in the dining room was marked with the company insignia. The letters BSPC are on the side of the sugar bowl and on the handles of the other pieces. Silver items like these are prized possessions of collectors today.

A portion of the *City of Richmond*'s dining room, which was located forward on the gallery deck, directly underneath the pilothouse. (*Photo by Hans Marx*)

Several members of the dining room and galley staff take a break in the *City of Richmond*'s galley. (*Photo by Hans Marx*)

8

On the Freight Deck

Although it is the passenger service of the Old Bay Line and Chesapeake Line that is best remembered, the shipment of freight was the real revenue producer for both lines for many years. It was sufficiently important that the Old Bay Line had a small fleet of steamers designed solely for the transportation of freight, but in the earliest days of steamboat operations, the carrying of passengers was of paramount importance and there was little room available for freight in the early boats.

That all changed by the mid-nineteenth century as the region grew and the demand for shipments of all kinds of freight by steamboat increased. To shippers, the steamboat was both safe and reliable. As steamers got larger and had more deck space, the main deck was given over almost completely to the carrying of bulk freight. Below that on the lower deck were the ship's holds, where even more freight could be carried. Eventually, the shipment of freight came to be measured in the hundreds of tons in the biggest steamers. Numerous steamboat lines operating out of Baltimore and Norfolk to landings on rivers like the Choptank, Patuxent, Nanticoke, Chester, York, and Rappahannock, provided a commercial lifeline to those rural areas and carried manufactured goods, medicine and clothing from the city, and vegetables, fruits, tobacco, seafood, and livestock from the rural wharves to the city.

The Baltimore–Norfolk steamers, however, were packets, meaning that they operated on a set schedule between those two cities with a brief stop at Old Point Comfort. They did not go up the rivers. Their freight consisted largely of shipments destined for clients in the two big cities and their surrounding areas, as well as freight to and from the railroads that owned the Old Bay Line and Chesapeake Line for transportation out of the area. There were also affiliated so-called "feeder lines" out of Norfolk such as those of the Old Dominion Line and the Virginia Navigation Company that carried freight and passengers that arrived from the big night boats. Much smaller vessels that could navigate the shallow Virginia rivers were used on these feeder lines.

Those feeder lines ran from Norfolk and Old Point Comfort to Richmond and wharves along the James River, to the Appomattox and Aquia rivers off the Potomac River, to the York River, and to small towns on Virginia's Eastern Shore such as Cherrystone. One of the busiest of the ports on the feeder lines was City Point, Virginia,

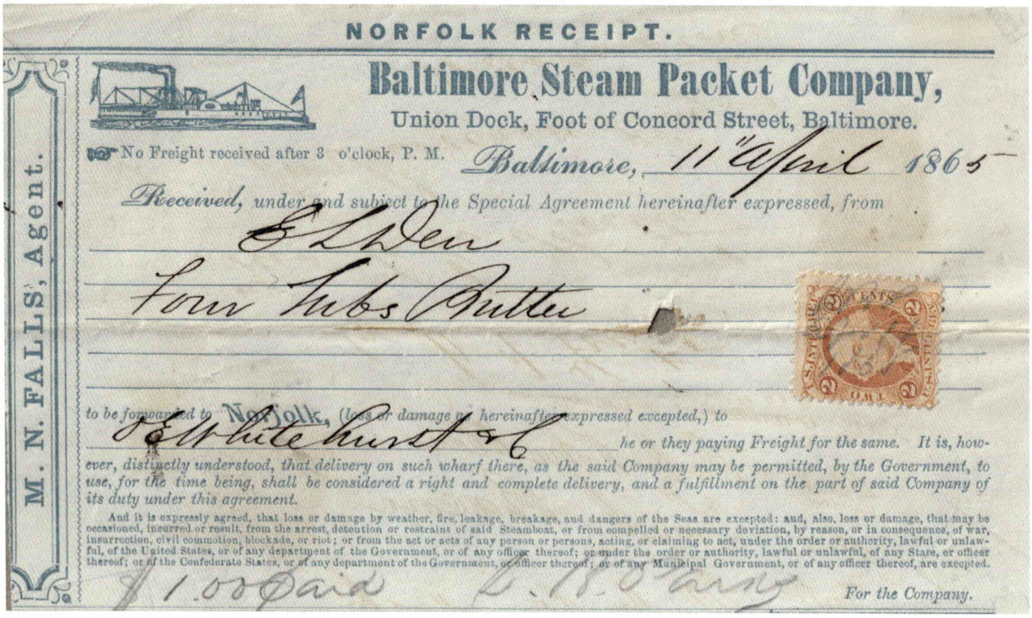

NORFOLK RECEIPT.

M. N. FALLS, Agent.

Baltimore Steam Packet Company,

Union Dock, Foot of Concord Street, Baltimore.

No Freight received after 3 o'clock, P. M. Baltimore, 186

Received, under and subject to the Special Agreement hereinafter expressed, from

to be forwarded to Norfolk, (loss or damage as hereinafter expressed excepted,) to

he or they paying Freight for the same. It is, however, distinctly understood, that delivery on such wharf there, as the said Company may be permitted, by the Government, to use, for the time being, shall be considered a right and complete delivery, and a fulfillment on the part of said Company of its duty under this agreement.

And it is expressly agreed, that loss or damage by weather, fire, leakage, breakage, and dangers of the Seas are excepted: and, also, loss or damage, that may be occasioned, incurred or result, from the arrest, detention or restraint of said Steamboat, or from compelled or necessary deviation, by reason, or in consequence, of war, insurrection, civil commotion, blockade, or riot; or from the act or acts of any person or persons, acting, or claiming to act, under the order or authority, lawful or unlawful, of the United States, or of any department of the Government, or of any officer thereof; or under the order or authority, lawful or unlawful, of any State, or officer thereof; or of the Confederate States, or of any department of the Government, or officer thereof; or of any Municipal Government, or of any officer thereof, are excepted.

For the Company.

A company freight receipt from April 11, 1865, covered the delivery of what appears to be four tubs of butter from Baltimore to Norfolk.

on the James River. By 1860, rail connections to the river wharves had improved and steamships—both inland water vessels and deep-sea steamers—were calling at City Point on·a regular basis.

When the Civil War broke out in 1861, the federal government provided plenty of freight business for the steamboat lines. As the Chesapeake Bay remained in Union hands throughout the war, the federal government made use of commercial steamers to carry war materiel, and one of the busiest ports was City Point. Much importance was attached to government contracts, especially the transportation of mail. The Bay Line was advertised as the only line carrying the United States Mail, Adams, and National Express shipments, and the only one that connected directly with the Seaboard and Roanoke Railroad, according to an undated advertisement.

Following the war, the shipment of commercial freight rapidly increased prompting the Old Bay Line to start running freight-only vessels that could go where the business was at any time (including up the rural rivers) without having to abide by pre-determined schedules. The first freight-only steamer acquired was the wooden-hull *New Jersey*, which had been built in 1862 in Newburgh, New York, and purchased by the Old Bay Line in 1867. She was obtained in a trade-in of the *Thomas A. Morgan* and cash. Although a small and rather inconspicuous wooden vessel, she was important in that she was the line's first propeller-driven steamer.

Following the acquisition of the *New Jersey*, the company added the wooden propeller-driven freighter *Transit*, and with these two vessels did a robust business transporting freight around the Bay and connecting with the river feeder lines. Unfortunately, the *New Jersey* burned on February 26, 1870, and both she and her cargo were a total loss.

The iron hull *Seaboard* was one of the company's first freight-only vessels. Her engines were aft, allowing for a considerable amount of freight to be carried on both the main and lower decks. (*Samuel Ward Stanton Collection, #MS0094/01-2464, Courtesy of the Mariners' Museum and Park.*)

In time, the company added the iron freighter *Roanoke* in 1871, the sister cargo ships *Westover* and *Shirley in* 1873, and the iron *Seaboard in* 1874, all built specifically for the Old Bay Line's flourishing freight-only operations. The *Seaboard* had a very long career under several owners well into the twentieth century. The *Shirley* and *Westover* operated primarily between Baltimore, Petersburg, and Richmond by way of Norfolk.

Larger and more efficient freighters were added when the wooden-hull *Raleigh* was built in 1873 and the iron *Gaston* in 1881. Even as late as 1881, the *Gaston* had three masts and carried auxiliary sails. With the advent of the newer freighters, the older ones were sold—the *Transit* went to New York and lasted until 1938, while the *Roanoke* found new owners on the Great Lakes and remained in service until 1906. The *Westover* was ultimately stranded in Florida in 1912, and the *Shirley* burned in Virginia in November 1880 only to be rebuilt and burn again a year later.

Other freighters operated over the years by the Old Bay Line included the *Alice* of 1845 on the James River route, the *Mount Vernon* of 1846 on the Appomattox River line, the *William Selden* of 1857, the freight and passenger steamer *Eolus* of 1864 on the feeder line from Norfolk to Cherrystone across the bay on Virginia's Eastern Shore, the *Cockade City of* 1863, and the second *Raleigh* of 1906, carrying general freight. The *Petersburg* of 1856 also carried general freight, and the *City of Philadelphia* was chartered briefly in 1904. The Chesapeake Line apparently never operated freight-only vessels.

The little *Eolus* appears to have been the only Old Bay Line ship to directly serve the Eastern Shore of Virginia. She left Norfolk for Cherrystone near Cape Charles at 6 a.m. on Monday, Wednesday, and Friday, calling at Old Point Comfort where freight and

The freighter *Gaston* had an iron hull and was built in 1881. Like other freighters in the fleet, she went wherever on the bay business took her. (*F.J. Sedgwick Collection, #MS0095/02-1160, Courtesy of the Mariners' Museum and Park*)

Built in 1906, the steel-hull *Raleigh* was the last freighter built for the company. She had especially fine lines and resembled a deep-sea freighter in many respects.

passengers from the overnight steamers from Baltimore could make the connection for the Eastern Shore. Arrival in Cherrystone and the nearby beaches was 10 a.m. The Baltimore boats also discharged freight at Old Point and it was transferred to feeder line steamers operating between Hampton Roads and Mobjack Bay in the lower Chesapeake.

The Old Bay Line, along with several other steamboat companies, reportedly established a freight service to Sharptown, Maryland, on the Nanticoke River on the Eastern Shore sometime around 1850, but the venture was short-lived. In Baltimore, there was an entity called the Canton Inside Line, which maintained a rail terminal in the Canton section of Baltimore's outer harbor. Old Bay Line freight steamers between Baltimore and Norfolk stopped there long enough to take on or unload freight and make connections with the Philadelphia, Wilmington & Baltimore Railroad, whose tracks came directly into Canton from the north. The Canton Inside Line operated until 1885.[1]

As larger passenger steamers with greater freight capacity joined the fleet in the 1880s and 1890s, the company had less need of cargo vessels but retained the *Seaboard* and the *Gaston* until 1920 to supplement the regular service. When the sister steamers *State of Maryland*, *State of Virginia*, and *President Warfield* came out in the 1920s, they had a freight capacity of 700 tons each, considerably more than earlier passenger steamers. Freight was carried on their main deck, the first one above the waterline, which was also called the freight deck. Freight was also carried in holds one deck below, which were loaded and unloaded with electric elevators in the later steamers.

The freight over the years was general in nature and often included such things as whiskey, flour, molasses, pig metal, slate, lumber, bricks, huge rolls of newsprint from southern paper mills, large spools of heavy-duty electrical cables, steel, copper, and other construction materials, various chemicals, tobacco fertilizer, tobacco compound, soap, sugar, and canned goods. Every once in a while, a casket destined for a funeral home or cemetery could be found on the freight manifest marked simply "corpse." Later, in the 1920s and 1930s, passengers' cars began sharing the freight deck with general freight. This constituted a trade-off, however, because the cars used space that would have been used for general freight. Unlike the small river steamers that called at rural ports where they picked up livestock for shipment to Baltimore, the Old Bay Line and Chesapeake Line steamers rarely, if ever, transported livestock.

Freight handling was very labor intensive and involved the drivers of the wagons and trucks that delivered the freight to the dock and picked it up, dock workers who took it on and off the ships with hand trucks or small motorized trucks moving pallets, and ships' officers monitoring the loading and unloading. As soon as the steamer was tied up, the three big cargo ports on the freight deck were opened, large loading ramps were run between ship and shore, and the freight began coming off or going on. It was a noisy business with the sounds of men and equipment filling the air. There were shouts from the officers overseeing the loading and unloading, the singing of the stevedores as they wrestled with the freight, and the rumbling across the ramp of the carts or trucks moving the freight between ship and shore. Every once in a while, an unusually heavy shipment was trundled on or off the steamer, causing her to briefly list, sometimes momentarily alarming passengers who were unaware of the activity on the freight deck and lower holds.

In Norfolk, after unloading passengers in the morning, the steamers would move about the harbor to the various marine terminals and to general freight terminals to load

Huge rolls of newsprint from paper mills in the south, seen here in the freight shed on Pier Three, Pratt Street, in Baltimore, were regularly shipped on the boats. (*Photo by Hans Marx*)

Electric trucks were used to unload some of the freight. This one is coming off the *City of Norfolk* in Baltimore. (*Photo by Hans Marx*)

Work crews operate electric elevators on a steamer's main deck. They were used to bring freight from the lower deck up to the main deck for classification before going to trucks waiting on the pier in Baltimore. (*Photo by Hans Marx*)

Old Bay Line covered barges known as lighters were moved by tugboats to and from freight customers in Baltimore harbor to pick up or deliver shipments. A small fleet of lighters is alongside the *City of Norfolk* at Pier Ten, Light Street. (*Photo by Hans Marx*)

and unload. They then returned to their regular berth in time to load passengers for the evening departure. In Baltimore, the freight was delivered to and picked up at the piers on Light Street and Pratt Street by trucks and barges known as lighters. In the 1950s the company maintained a fleet of fourteen covered lighters. It was not uncommon at that time for several tractor trailers to be on Pier Three at the same time, loading and unloading.

"The value of rail-water service to the shipping public depends largely upon the ability of that service to charge lower rates than assessed by other modes of transportation between the same points," the Old Bay Line stated in a freight circular. Bay Line officials maintained for many years that domestic shipping could move freight cheaper than other modes of transport.

The only other instance of the company owning a freight-only boat was in 1936 when it acquired the diesel-powered *Alcyone* largely for charter purposes. She had originally been built in 1907 as a luxury steam yacht and was converted for commercial use in 1935. She remained on the roster until sold in 1941.

As passenger service declined with the national infatuation with the automobile after World War II, it was freight operations that proved to be the breadwinner for the by-then merged Old Bay Line and Chesapeake Line. Then, in 1955, a series of strikes disrupted operations and a number of longtime freight customers sought other carriers, and never returned to the Bay Line. Nevertheless, the line's railroad owners apparently considered the freight connection in Baltimore to be of sufficient importance to keep the line going, and did so until 1962.

Above left: Pier Three, Pratt Street, in Baltimore was large enough to handle a number of tractor-trailers at once, making for an efficient transfer of freight. (*Photo by Hans Marx*)

Above right: In Norfolk, the steamers made the rounds of the various marine terminals during the day to pick up and discharge freight. Here is the *City of Norfolk* at the Lambert's Point terminal of the Norfolk and Western Railway.

9

"When We Left, It Was Just a Fresh Breeze"

Chesapeake Bay night boats were not ferries, nor were they excursion boats or cruise ships. They were staunch passenger and freight ships that sailed on a daily basis year-round between Baltimore and Norfolk, and they rarely missed a sailing because of weather. Simply put, they went in just about all kinds of weather within reason, and on the evening of August 23, 1933, there was no reason to suppose that the Old Bay Line's *State of Maryland* and the Chesapeake Line's *City of Norfolk* would not depart from Baltimore on schedule.

Northeast winds were in the forecast but neither Captain John L. Marshall of the *State of Maryland* nor Captain Edward James of the *City of Norfolk* had any cause for concern because there was no mention of severe weather in the forecast for Chesapeake Bay. From all appearances, the weather looked to be no worse than the many nor'easters these veteran seamen had steamed through for so many years without difficulty.

"There were no storm warnings at all. Nobody told us a storm was approaching. When we left, it was just a fresh breeze," Patrick L. Parker, first mate on the *State of Maryland* said many years later.[1] So, promptly at 6:30 p.m., the two steamers pulled away from their Light Street docks and headed for the open bay.

Meanwhile, 325 miles to the south, a hurricane that many thought would only brush the Mid-Atlantic coast, if that, came ashore on the Outer Banks of North Carolina. It was the eighth storm of the 1933 hurricane season, which would turn out to be the most active season up to that time. It had formed near the Cape Verde Islands off the west coast of Africa on August 17 and moved west across the Atlantic. After hitting the Outer Banks, the storm passed over Norfolk, Virginia, and turned and headed up the western shore of Chesapeake Bay. It had sustained winds of between 75 and 82 miles per hour with higher gusts and was also a prodigious rainmaker. It was into this maelstrom that the *State of Maryland* and *City of Norfolk* steamed in the early morning hours of August 24.

Except for some mild rolling and gusty winds, all was well on the two night boats at first, but then, conditions unexpectedly began to worsen after midnight. The wind rapidly increased and whipped the waters of the bay into a frenzy. When Patrick Parker came on watch at midnight, he was amazed at how much the weather had worsened. "The further down the Bay we went, the worse it got. We still didn't realize it was a hurricane," he recalled.[2]

By this time, the two steamers were just above Wolf Trap Light near the entrance to the Rappahannock River, but they could not see the lighthouse or any other navigation aids because of the blinding rain. The *State of Maryland* plowed on into the night, but the *City of Norfolk*, which was some distance behind the *Maryland*, was in trouble. Shortly after 1 a.m. a huge sea slammed into the *Norfolk*'s port quarter and tore off one of the large side cargo ports and the vessel began to take on water with each additional big wave. Although attempting to turn in such conditions was not only difficult but dangerous, Captain James felt he had no other choice.[3]

With great difficulty, the *City of Norfolk* came around into the wind and stayed as steady as possible in that position while keeping the damaged cargo port away from the oncoming seas. This worked for several hours but with the wind and high seas continuing to pound the ship, Captain James decided to try and find a suitable place to anchor. However, when the anchors were dropped and they failed to hold the steamer, they were brought back aboard and there were just two anchor chains without anchors. The chains had apparently parted and there were two 3,000-lb anchors sitting somewhere on the bottom.

Shortly after noon, the *City of Norfolk* went aground on the Watts Island Flats at the western edge of Pocomoke Sound far from her regular route in the shipping channel, and there she stayed. Fortunately, the bottom of the bay is mostly mud and sand so she was not damaged by the grounding. She had no radio and was unable to summon any help. She would have to wait until the storm subsided before she could expect assistance.

Meanwhile, the *State of Maryland* continued south but it was tough going. She was rolling heavily from side to side but was able to remain on course. She too was getting slammed by big waves, but did not sustain the kind of damage the *City of Norfolk* did. However, several railings were torn off as were some lifeboat covers but there was no serious damage.

Captain Marshall hoped he could get the steamer alongside the Old Point Comfort wharf but it was too exposed and the wind was too strong to allow the 330-foot vessel to make it, so she continued on her way to Norfolk.

Although the wind continued to rage, the high seas had dissipated somewhat as the steamer approached the Old Bay Line wharf at the foot of Main Street. The water, however, covered the dock and the entire surrounding area, hampering efforts to get the lines ashore because the line handlers were working in waist-deep water. For Captain Marshall, it was difficult work but he finally succeeded in getting her alongside. Much of downtown Norfolk was under several feet of water so most of the passengers decided to remain aboard until the storm had passed. The unloading of freight would obviously have to wait since the wharf warehouse was also flooded.

Then, around 9 a.m., the wind shifted, indicating that the worst of the storm had passed. "You could almost see the tide going down," said Patrick Parker.[4] Captain Marshall called it the worst storm he had been through in eighteen years at sea.

The *City of Norfolk*, however, which would normally have docked at about the same time, was nowhere to be seen and nothing had been heard from her. By 2 a.m. on August 25, there was still no word, and concern was growing.

Out on the Watts Island Flats, all the *City of Norfolk's* passengers and crew could do was wait. Finally, around 1:30 p.m., a plane from the Naval Air Station in Norfolk sighted the grounded steamer. She had been missing for thirty hours.

Despite what the steamer had been through, no one was hurt. On the morning of August 26, the *Norfolk*'s sister ship, the *City of Baltimore* arrived on the scene to take the passengers off the stranded vessel. As the water was so shallow, the *City of Baltimore* had to remain 2 miles away in deep water while the *City of Norfolk*'s lifeboats were used to transfer her fifty-two passengers to her sister ship, which took them to Norfolk.

The *City of Norfolk* remained aground for a month while a channel was dredged to get her back to deep water with the help of pontoons. During that time, she had to endure another severe storm that swept the area on September 15 but managed to ride it out with no damage. She finally returned to service on October 20.

The storm turned out to be the most severe one to hit the region since 1821. At least one oceangoing passenger and freight ship off the Maryland coast reported being hit by a rogue sea during the storm that did major damage to the vessel. There was widespread damage in Maryland and Virginia, and the storm cut a new inlet to the ocean at Ocean City, Maryland. It destroyed dozens of steamboat wharves along the bay and its tributaries. Damages in both states was in the multi-millions. Not until 2003 when Hurricane Isabel followed a similar track was there a storm to match what became known as the Chesapeake and Potomac Hurricane of August 1933.

10

An Anniversary and a Merger

As the 1930s drew to a close, the Old Bay Line and the Chesapeake Line faced a dilemma. As they had since the 1890s, the competing companies were continuing to send their steamers forth every evening—four large vessels for the Baltimore–Norfolk line and one vessel for Chesapeake's York River service. However, the steamers were operating at a deficit and were making their nightly sailings with many empty staterooms and half-full freight decks, thanks to the economic climate of the 1930s.

The problem was not unique to Chesapeake Bay. Inland and coastal steamship lines up and down the East Coast were feeling the effects of the depression and trucks and automobiles that were taking away a big chunk of their business, as did labor issues. Some did not survive the decade. In the case of the Old Bay Line, it had only two profitable years in the 1930s and ran up a sizeable deficit for the decade. Accountants for the Chesapeake Line were dealing with even worse numbers and did not see the situation improving. It reached the point that the two railroads that owned the Chesapeake Line were unwilling to continue throwing good money after bad and urged that the two steamboat lines merge.

Therefore, on April 16, 1940, the Old Bay Line filed a merger application in the Federal Court in Norfolk for it to take over the Chesapeake Line. The two companies had discussed merging several times during the late 1930s but were never able to reach an agreement. This time, however, the very survival of overnight steamship operations between Baltimore and Norfolk was at stake. There simply was not enough business for both companies to remain solvent if things continued in the same fashion. Backers of the merger were convinced that a combined company could make money and erase the deficits.

In testimony before the Interstate Commerce Commission, Old Bay Line Vice President Robert E. Dunn said a merged company could save a total of $205,000 in annual operating expenses, including savings of $74,000 in steamer operation, $40,000 in terminal expenses, and $30,000 by doing away with duplicate office staffs. It was estimated that about seventy-seven positions would be eliminated resulting in significant savings.

Merger negotiations were complicated, however, by the fact that the Old Bay Line's parent company—the Seaboard Air Line Railway—was nearing the end of a lengthy period of receivership, and approval by the court was necessary, in addition to approval by the Interstate Commerce Commission. As a result, it would be more than a year before the merger would be completed, assuming all went well.

Meanwhile, a major celebration was planned for the Old Bay Line, which turned 100 years old on May 23, 1940. It was a gala affair at both ends of the bay, involving parades, dinners, governors, mayors, steamship company officials, and actors in nineteenth century attire. Before the flagship *President Warfield* cast off from Baltimore, however, there was much merriment.

It began with a parade that started at Baltimore's Lord Baltimore Hotel, featuring open carriages with the mayor of Baltimore, the governor of Maryland, and the mayors and city managers of Norfolk, Portsmouth, Newport News, and Hampton, Virginia. It wound its way through downtown, finally coming to a stop outside the Old Bay Line's home at Pier Ten, Light Street, which was festooned with flags, banners, and signs proclaiming the anniversary. Cars and trucks blew their horns and streetcars rang their bells, and no one really seemed to mind the crowd that milled about on Light Street.

Aboard the *President Warfield*, a gala Centennial Dinner was served that featured, among other delicacies, seafood cocktail, terrapin *à la* Chesapeake, and roast golden pheasant, each course accompanied by a different wine and followed by desserts of jubilee ice cream, fancy cakes, and a special moche, a dessert made from rice, caramel grated coconut, and other ingredients.

Throughout the meal, musicians in nineteenth-century attire serenaded the diners. The *Warfield* finally cast off later that evening, and during the trip down to Norfolk, a pageant with costumed actors was staged in the social hall, recalling key moments in the company's history, and a cake covered with candles was cut by Maryland Governor Herbert R. O'Conor. Many of the revelers danced to the orchestra well into the early morning hours.

The observances continued after the steamer reached Norfolk, with an ongoing celebration at the Cavalier Hotel in nearby Virginia Beach. The day was capped by another gala dinner after which the *Warfield* and her special guests returned to Baltimore.

Completion of the merger was still nearly a year away at the time of the centennial, but finally on April 16, 1941, the Interstate Commerce Commission gave its blessing. On May 29, Federal Judge Luther Way in Norfolk gave the necessary legal approval for the merger to proceed, bringing to an end forty-five years of often heated competition between the two lines. The combined company now had three railroad owners—the Seaboard Air Line owned half, the Southern Railway one-third, and the Atlantic Coast Line one-sixth.

The merger gave the Old Bay Line six steamers—the *President Warfield*, *State of Maryland*, *State of Virginia*, *Yorktown*, *City of Norfolk*, and *City of Richmond*. The plan was for the four newest ships to operate daily in the Baltimore–Norfolk trade, two of which would carry passengers only while the other two carried freight only. One steamer—the *City of Richmond*—was to continue on the York River Line for the time being with passengers and freight for Richmond two or three times a week as traffic dictated. She also ran weekend houseboat cruises in 1941 when not on the York River. The *City of Norfolk*, the oldest vessel in the fleet, was held in reserve as a spare steamer, according to Captain Patrick L. Parker. In fact, the line anticipated retiring the *City of Norfolk* and *City of Richmond*, which were considerably older than the other four ships.

Colorful advertisements were published by the Old Bay Line to call attention to its centennial in 1940.

The Old Bay Line put on a big celebration on May 23, 1940, observing the company's 100th anniversary. Pier Ten, Light Street, was suitably decorated for the occasion. (*Photo by Hans Marx*)

Above left: Maryland Governor Herbert R. O'Conor (center) took part by cutting the centennial cake. At left is company vice-president Robert E. Dunn and second from the right is the *Warfield*'s social directress Louise Lazenby. (*Photo by Hans Marx*)

Above right: Colorful skits featuring actors in nineteenth-century garb took place on the *President Warfield* as she steamed down the bay, recalling key moments in the line's history. (*Photo by Hans Marx*)

Below: The celebration continued on the *Warfield*'s open decks. Re-enactors crowd the steamer's foredeck to continue their skits about the line's century of operations. (*Photo by Hans Marx*)

The merry-making went on after the *Warfield* reached Norfolk and into the evening as she prepared to depart for Baltimore. (*Photo by Hans Marx*)

As music played and sung by the various actors resonated across the harbor, the *President Warfield* departed from Norfolk on the evening of May 25, bringing down the curtain on the centennial celebration.

Colorful souvenir plates were created for the centennial celebration, depicting representative vessels of the company as well as imagery of the line's route between Baltimore and Norfolk.

During the time the merger was being consummated, however, both passenger and freight business was dramatically increasing as a result of the national defense buildup. Where freight decks had once been half empty, they were filled with freight, much of it military in nature, bound for Hampton Roads. As so many service personnel and government officials were also bound for the military establishments around Hampton Roads, passenger accommodations filled up rapidly.

On June 25, 1941, Robert E. Dunn was named president of the Old Bay Line, having served as vice president since 1934. As he took over, he must have been pleased with the upsurge in business and the knowledge that the line now had a sizeable fleet with which to deliver the goods. Little did he know that the company was about to enter one of the most difficult periods in its history.

11

Called Up for War Service

With the tremendous increase in business, the Old Bay Line needed to reactivate the *City of Norfolk*, giving the company five steamers with which to handle the demand for freight and passenger space. All of them were put to work carrying both passengers and freight. That worked out to about 2,000 passengers per voyage on all five steamers and several hundred tons of freight down below. This meant a dramatic increase in revenue for the company after the lean years of the 1930s.

Passenger traffic on the York River Line, however, had been falling off for some time, and the decision was made to shut down the passenger side of the business, ending a service that had existed in one form or another since the mid-nineteenth century. Freight-only business continued with three-times-a-week departures through the first few months of 1941, and on at least one occasion, the *City of Richmond* sailed from Baltimore to West Point by way of Norfolk, according to log books that have survived. But shortly afterward, it was decided to end the York River Line completely, and on July 11, 1941, the *City of Richmond* sailed for the last time from West Point.[1]

> The last boat ... was a poignant occasion for many of the residents of West Point. As the *City of Richmond* steamed down the York, A.T. Donnell, the local agent, stood with a group on the wharf and gazed for quite a while until the boat was out of sight.[2]

The fact that the York River service did not appear in the Old Bay Line's 1942 brochure suggests that its days were already numbered.

Old Bay Line steamers had played various roles in the Civil War and World War I, and it was expected that they would do so again in like fashion this time—providing much needed transportation up and down Chesapeake Bay. In 1942, however, the Old Bay Line's contribution to the war effort was much different.

The company was notified by the War Shipping Administration that it was requisitioning the *State of Virginia* for war service on April 1, 1942. As if that was not enough of a shock for the company, it was informed the next day that the *State of Maryland* was also being requisitioned. No details were given as to the government's plans for the sister ships.

As soon as they became government property, the *State of Maryland* and *State of Virginia* went off to be converted for war service. The *Maryland* was taken to the Baltimore yard of the Maryland Shipbuilding and Drydock Company, and the *Virginia* went to the Newport News Shipbuilding and Drydock Company in Virginia. The conversion was startling. The three top decks were extensively altered and a new superstructure with a lower profile took their place. Steel plating was added to enclose the sides of what had been the saloon deck. The forward end of the superstructure was squared off like that of an ocean-going ship, gun tubs were located on either side of the wheelhouse, and a cluster of cargo booms was erected forward.

Inside, dormitory-style troop accommodations occupied the better part of what had once been the gallery deck, and a hospital was located aft on that deck. Freight was carried on the main deck and in the lower deck holds. Refrigerated cargo space was expanded, and both oil and water capacity were increased. Once the conversion work was completed, they were commissioned as the U.S. Army transports *State of Maryland* and *State of Virginia* to be operated by the Army Transportation Corps in the Antilles Department in the Caribbean. They were capable of carrying up to 583 troops. The *Maryland*'s crew consisted of three military officers and twenty-eight enlisted men, as well as fourteen licensed and eighty-five unlicensed civilians; on the *Virginia*, there were two military officers and twenty-eight enlisted men, along with fourteen licensed and eighty-five unlicensed civilians.

They would never again sail for the Old Bay Line.

The company was fortunate to have had a fleet of six vessels following the merger, and no sooner had two of them been taken away than Dunn stated that the company would continue regular service with the four vessels that remained. It would, however, almost certainly mean even more overcrowding and discomfort in the passenger spaces and more people and freight left on the dock because there was no more room on the steamers. Service between Baltimore and Norfolk continued with the *President Warfield*, *Yorktown*, *City of Norfolk*, and *City of Richmond*. There was no longer anymore talk of retiring the two oldest former Chesapeake Line ships.

Then came another shock. On July 11 and 12 came word that the *President Warfield* and *Yorktown* were also being requisitioned. The government, which also took over at the same time the *Northland* and *Southland* of the Norfolk and Washington Steamboat Company and the *Virginia Lee* of the Pennsylvania Railroad route across the mouth of the bay, would only say that they were required for war service. This was a stunning blow for the Old Bay Line, which, in the space of a little more than three months, went from a six-ship company to a two-ship company. It was left to operate in the busiest period in its history with the thirty-one-year-old *City of Norfolk* and twenty-nine-year-old *City of Richmond* and had no third steamer available in case one of the other two had to be taken out of service temporarily. The company put on a brave face and promised that service would continue as before. The *President Warfield* and *Yorktown*, meanwhile, were being prepared for adventures on the high seas that no one could ever have imagined.

Within hours of the government takeover of the vessels, crews from the Maryland Shipbuilding and Drydock Company went to work on preparing them for war service. While they did not undergo the radical exterior changes that the *State of Maryland* and *State of Virginia* did, their interiors underwent a major transformation. All but four staterooms on the saloon deck were removed, creating a large open space for a troop dormitory. Most staterooms on the gallery deck remained, along with many on the hurricane deck. A gunnery platform equipped with a 12-pounder was installed at the cut-down after end of the saloon deck. Gun tubs with 20-mm Oerlikons were added near the funnels and wheelhouses.

Above: The *State of Maryland* and *State of Virginia* were radically altered in appearance and became troop transports and cargo vessels in the Caribbean Theatre during the war. This is the U.S. Army Transport *State of Virginia* at an unidentified location. (*National Archives and Records Administration, MISC 232442*)

Left: The *President Warfield* arrives in Baltimore for the last time as an Old Bay Line ship on May 11, 1942. The next day, she and the *Yorktown* were officially requisitioned for war service. (*Photo by Hans Marx*)

The *City of Norfolk*, acquired in the 1941 merger, was the oldest vessel in the fleet, having been built in 1911. She had been earmarked for scrapping but was called on to serve in the absence of the four newer vessels.

The 1913-built *City of Richmond,* also scheduled for scrapping, teamed with the *City of Norfolk* to carry on the Old Bay Line's service with no backup steamer in case of emergencies. They almost always carried overflow crowds during the war.

Heavy wood planking covered the windows and other openings of the saloon deck along with the open part of the main deck at the stern. To protect against heavy seas coming over the bow, a heavy wooden turtleback covered the foredeck almost up to the wheelhouse. Captain Patrick L. Parker, the *Warfield*'s last Old Bay Line master, and Chief Engineer C. M. "Skeeter" Walker were assigned as liaisons to assist with the conversion.

These preparations were necessary because the *Warfield* and *Yorktown* and a number of other coastal and inland steamers were being turned over to the British and were being readied for a voyage across the stormy North Atlantic. As part of the United States' Lend-Lease Program, the ships were provided to Britain for use as transports, training vessels, hospital ships, and accommodation vessels around Britain. The plan was to get them across the Atlantic before heavy weather set in. Volunteer British crews were brought over to the U.S. on the *Queen Mary* but knew only that they were embarking on a special mission.

"Our first thought when we saw it, we really wondered what we were looking at. It looked so odd with all the heavy wood that had been put up in the superstructure," said John Winter, second radio operator on the *Yorktown*. "One of the first things we said, having been at sea, was that this thing's going to roll like a tub, and it did."[3]

At about the same time a continent away, two former Old Bay Line steamers were also being called up for military service. The former *Alabama* of 1892, after operating for a number of years on Puget Sound as the ferry *City of Victoria*, became a floating dormitory for workers building a new naval base in Sitka, Alaska. She provided similar service for the Navy during the war and was scrapped in 1948. The former *Florida* of 1907, which had been a ferry on San Francisco Bay, joined the navy as a floating barracks dubbed YFB-21 at Mare Island and served through the war.

The *President Warfield* and *Yorktown* sailed from Baltimore on August 20, 1942, along with several of the other requisitioned steamers for New York, the first stop on their way to St. John's, Newfoundland, where a convoy was to be formed for the open sea voyage. Many years later, Captain Parker said being part of the conversion process was difficult for him.

"We also went with the ships to New York, we were [asked] to go as far as Halifax, but by that time we had had enough and was ready to return to the Bay Line," he said.[4]

The *President Warfield* and *Yorktown* were sent across the Atlantic in convoy with several other coastal steamers. This is how the *Yorktown* looked after conversion with heavy wooden timbers and planking providing protection against heavy seas. (*National Archives and Records Administration*)

At about the same time, the former Old Bay Liner *Florida* of 1907, which had been a west coast ferry for many years, was acquired by the navy for government service as an accommodation ship at Mare Island, California.

Back in Baltimore, he was given command of the *City of Norfolk*, a position he would hold for twenty years.

It turned out that the *Virginia Lee* and the Baltimore–Philadelphia night boat *John Cadwalader*, another steamer scheduled to cross with the convoy, were unable to make the crossing, so joining the *Warfield*, *Yorktown*, *Northland*, and *Southland* for the trip across the ocean were the sister ships *Boston* and *New York* of the Eastern Steamship Company's New York–Boston run, and the *Naushon* and *New Bedford* of the New England Steamship Company's service to Nantucket Island and Martha's Vineyard. Along with two Royal Navy destroyers, the *Veteran* and the *Vanoc*, Convoy RB-1 (the RB was said to stand for river boat), headed out to sea on September 21, 1942, bound for a stop in Iceland before going on to Scotland. Dark humor attended its departure, with names like "convoy maniac," "skimming dishes," and "the honeymoon fleet" being applied to what must have been one of the most unusual convoys ever to put to sea in wartime.

Rough seas accompanied the steamers for the first four days—8- and 9-foot seas and very high winds, Winter recalled—and there were various reports of a German surface raider and several submarines in the area. Lookouts were intently scanning the sea for any sign of the enemy. The ships rolled constantly and crew members found it increasingly difficult to remain in their bunks. The convoy was steaming at between ten and fifteen knots. There was no sign of the enemy into the morning of the fifth day, September 25, which was sunny and not quite as rough. Confidence began to build that perhaps this odd little convoy might just make it safely across the Atlantic.

Then, without warning in the early afternoon, there was a tremendous explosion as two torpedoes ripped into the side of the convoy commodore's flagship *Boston*. Within moments, she reared her bow into the air and slipped from sight. Pandemonium broke out among the other vessels as the *New Bedford* and *Northland* moved in to pick up survivors. A surfaced submarine was sighted nearby and a periscope from another

U-boat was seen near the *Southland*, which opened up with her twelve-pounder. The sub disappeared, only to be followed by another. The *President Warfield* had to take evasive action within minutes to avoid a torpedo sent her way. It passed by only about 30 feet away, but another periscope was sighted not far off, and the *Warfield*, with the help of the *Veteran*, opened fire and the periscope disappeared.

At least five submarines—*U-216*, *U-96*, *U-91*, *U-404*, and *U-619*—continued to harass the now-scattered convoy until shortly before midnight when the *New York*, the vice-commodore's ship, was hit by a torpedo and erupted in flames. As the mortally-wounded steamer wallowed in the swells, the *Veteran* came up to rescue men in the water and was herself hit by a German torpedo. The *Veteran* went down quickly, taking not only her entire complement, but many of those she had rescued. The *New York* remained afloat until very early on the morning of the sixth day when a torpedo from *U-404* finished her off.[5]

By this time, the six remaining steamers had scattered in hopes of shaking off the U-boats. The decision was made to try and reach mainland ports independently without making the stop in Iceland. The sea was kicking up again and the steamers found the going rough. The *Yorktown* was steaming out of sight of the other vessels late in the afternoon of September 26 when steering problems developed, forcing her to stop and become a sitting duck while repairs were made. Once repairs had been completed, she resumed her course, hoping to make it to Ireland or Scotland in another day or two, but it was not to be.

Shortly before 9 p.m. with no warning, a torpedo fired by *U-619* slammed into the port side of the former Old Bay Liner. John Winter said he and Captain W.P Boylan were chatting in the radio operator's cabin when it happened. Winter remembered:

> I was sitting ... on the bunk when the torpedo hit ... Captain Boylan was standing on the deck and the entire inside of the ship just collapsed. Then I slipped off the bunk ... and fell a considerable distance although I was not injured in any way, and I heard Captain Boylan saying "Come on, let's get out of here. Get out where you can see the light."

In the rapidly waning light of day, the two men swam away from the ship and could see others in the water nearby. They looked back at the *Yorktown* and saw "a tremendous hole" perhaps 20 feet across where the forward portion of the ship's wooden portside had been. From the funnel aft, the ship seemed "pretty well intact," Winter said.[6]

Within minutes—some accounts said only three minutes—the *Yorktown* settled and disappeared beneath the rolling waves. Several rafts had come loose when the ship sank, and the survivors crawled aboard only to endure forty-six more hours in heavy seas, high winds, and cold until the destroyer *Sardonyx* picked them up.

Not aware of the disaster that had befallen the *Yorktown*, the remaining members of the convoy steamed on, finally arriving in various ports on their own without further mishap. The *President Warfield* reached Belfast, the *Naushon* and *Northland* made it to Londonderry, and the *Southland* and *New Bedford* made port in Greenock on the Clyde.

Over 130 seamen lost their lives in the attacks on Convoy RB-1, attacks that German reports claimed sank several ships "of the *Queen Mary* class," mentioning as possible victims the liners *Reina del Pacifico*, *Derbyshire*, and *Viceroy of India*. The reports also said that the defense had been "so fierce that it could not be observed whether two or more of the transports hit sank or not" and that "our submarines have dealt a heavy blow at the enemy."[7]

By the KING'S Order the name of
William John Charles Winter, Esq.
Second Radio Officer, s.s. Yorktown,
was published in the London Gazette on
11 May, 1943.
as commended for brave conduct in the
Merchant Navy.
I am charged to record His Majesty's
high appreciation of the service rendered.

Winston S. Churchill

Prime Minister and First Lord
of the Treasury

Above left: The *Yorktown* was torpedoed and sunk in the North Atlantic and her survivors had to endure forty-eight hours in lifeboats and rafts in high seas before being rescued. (*Courtesy of John Winter*)

Above right: John Winter of the *Yorktown* was among the surviving officers of Convoy RB-1 to receive a commendation from King George VI by way of Prime Minister Winston Churchill. (*Courtesy of John Winter*)

Although it was initially believed that one or more submarines were damaged or sunk in the attacks, German records show that there were no submarine casualties. Special commendations were awarded to a number of the surviving ships' officers by King George VI and there were a number of posthumous awards as well. It has been suggested by some over the years that Convoy RB-1 was a decoy convoy, designed to draw German submarines away from a more important troop convoy headed for North Africa. That has never been proven, but it would seem that these unlikely "warships" were, indeed, needed in the waters around the British Isles. Had they simply been decoys, the surviving vessels might have been shunted aside unused once they made port, but they were all immediately put to work doing the duties, which were outlined for them when they were first called up.

The *President Warfield* was initially designated as a hospital carrier, but those plans were shelved for unknown reasons and she was sent to the village of Appledore on the Torridge River in Devon, England. There, under charter to the British Ministry of War Transport, she was run hard aground and served until mid-April 1944 as a barracks and accommodation ship for the training of hundreds of amphibious units preparing for the invasion of Europe. The *Northland* and *Southland* saw service as transports, carrying military personnel to various locations throughout Britain. They also carried military cargo. All three of these former American steamers were well-suited to these kinds of operations because of their shallow draft, which was usually around 15 feet.

The *Naushon* and *New Bedford* were converted to hospital ships—hospital carriers in British lexicon—and also trained for duty in the invasion of Europe. Here again, shallow draft played an important part—these hospital ships could come in and practically touch the beach, which they did on June 6, 1944, when Allied forces invaded France. Prior to D-Day, however, the *President Warfield*, *Northland*, and *Southland* were turned over to the U.S. Navy to become part of American operations along the Normandy beaches. The two former Norfolk–Washington boats continued to see service as transports but a higher calling awaited the *Warfield*.

On July 6, she steamed across the English Channel to the manmade harbor at Omaha Beach. She became the headquarters ship for the American forces at Omaha Beach. Undoubtedly, the military brass that came to live aboard appreciated her remaining staterooms, some still with the original peacetime beds and baths. She remained in that role until November 14, 1944, and then was assigned to carry troops on the River Seine between Le Havre and Rouen, France.

After several months in that service, she was ordered on July 3, 1945, to a French dry dock to prepare for a voyage home across the Atlantic. The *Southland* and *Northland*, however, were not returned to the United States because it was felt that at their age (built 1908 and 1911 respectively), they were not up to another transatlantic crossing. Instead, they were eventually sold to Chinese buyers and managed to steam all the way to Hong Kong—without any problems at all—where they entered service as riverboats on Chinese rivers. They were reportedly scrapped in 1955.

Meanwhile, in the army's Antilles Department in the Caribbean, the *State of Maryland* and *State of Virginia* spent the war years providing reliable and much-needed if unspectacular service transporting troops and military cargo. The island bases in the Antilles Department were used by forces being trained for defense operations, construction and maintenance, and tactical air and ground training. Puerto Rico and many other islands were part of the department. Wartime records show the two former Old Bay Liners shuttling back and forth between such ports as San Juan, Curacao, Aruba, Cristobal, and Port of Spain. Their shuttle operations occasionally took them to mainland Ports of Embarkation such as New Orleans and Charleston, South Carolina. Wartime records show that perhaps the most exciting thing to happen to either of them was in March 1943 when the *State of Maryland* ran hard aground off Cape Haitien.[8]

The *State of Maryland* was still on duty in the Caribbean as of January 1946, records show. She was decommissioned and placed in the Mobile, Alabama Reserve Fleet on September 4, 1946, where she was later described as barely afloat. She was sold for scrap in 1950 in Mobile. The *State of Virginia* remained on duty through the end of 1945 and was placed in the Mobile Reserve Fleet on February 18, 1947. She was scrapped in Baltimore in 1952.[9]

While the *President Warfield*, *State of Maryland*, and *State of Virginia* went about their military duties, the *City of Norfolk* and *City of Richmond* were doing their best to maintain the company's nightly passenger and freight business. They were overwhelmed night after night with passengers—many of them military—and quantities of freight that taxed the capacity of the freight deck and cargo holds. All domestic steamship lines were finding it difficult not only to maintain overworked vessels in serviceable condition but were also frustrated by the inability to maintain crews and dock workers since most able-bodied young

The U.S.S. *President Warfield* was used by the Navy as a headquarters and barracks ship at Omaha Beach, a month after D-Day. She was popular because she still had a few peacetime accommodations on board. (*U.S. Navy photo by Machinist's Mate First Class Kenneth Waters, U.S. Naval History and Heritage Command*)

Following her duty at Omaha Beach, the *Warfield* was sent to France where she carried troops on the Seine River between Le Havre and Rouen. (*David C. Holly collection, Calvert Marine Museum*)

men were off at war. It is a credit to the management of the Old Bay Line and the steamers' officers that they were able to maintain a credible service in the face of such adversity.

The *City of Norfolk* and *City of Richmond* were driven hard, and it was impossible to take either out of service for much-needed maintenance and repairs since the company did not have a backup steamer. Military personnel were given preference for tickets, accommodations, and meals. The evening meal went well into the night. Civilian travelers had to wait and hope space and food was still available for them.[10]

A company official was stationed at the gangway counting passengers coming on board, and when a certain number was reached, loading stopped. When all the staterooms were filled, many passengers fended for themselves as best they could, sleeping on chairs and couches in the lounges, or deck chairs on the exterior decks. Mothers tried to get babies to sleep in their laps.

Each vessel carried an armed Naval Shore Patrol contingent whose job it was to keep the military personnel organized. When 10 p.m. came, the Shore Patrol, along with the captain and the ship's watchman, circulated through the vessel and told everyone in uniform that it was time for bed. All lights in public spaces except for necessary saloon lights were turned off.

Somehow, it all worked, and the company came through its most trying time without any major mishaps. Yet it desperately needed a third boat so its two over-taxed steamers could get long-deferred maintenance.

Finally, the War Shipping Administration agreed to charter the steamer *Meteor*, a veteran of Long Island Sound service, to the Old Bay Line. Built in 1899 at Sparrows Point, the

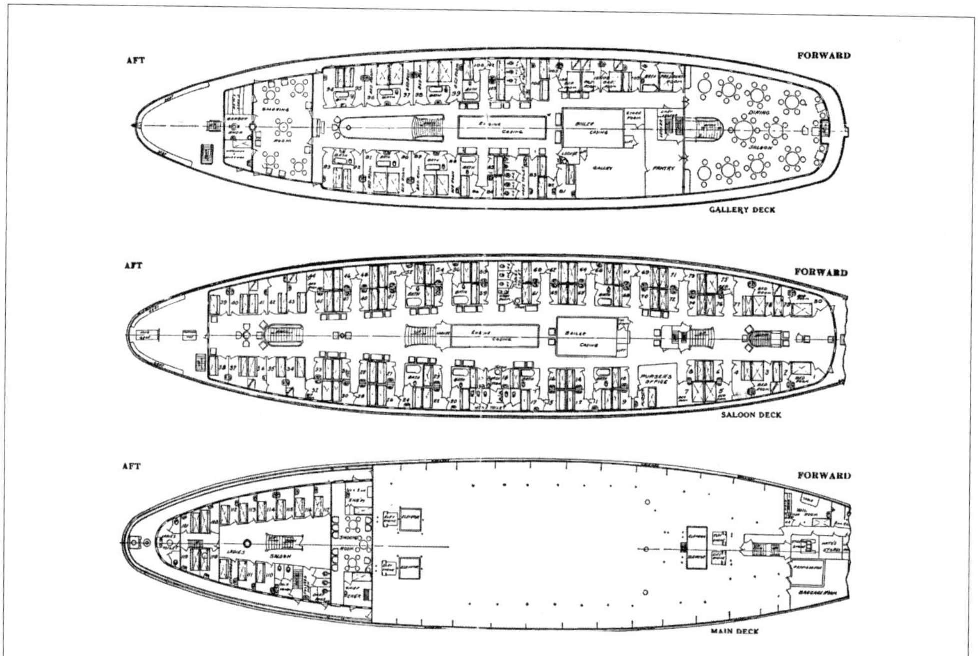

The stateroom accommodation plan for the *City of Richmond*. The large open space on the Main Deck was where freight was carried. Freight was also carried one deck below on the lower deck.

Meteor was a little larger than the *City of Norfolk* and *City of Richmond*, and, like the other Old Bay Line steamers, had been requisitioned in 1942, but was not significantly altered. She most recently served as a receiving station ship for the army. Before she could go into service for the Bay Line, however, she underwent $800,000 worth of renovations and then made her first run down the Bay on March 7, 1944.

By that time, space had finally become available in shipyards for commercial vessels to undergo repairs. The timing couldn't have been better and with the *Meteor* in service, the *City of Richmond* was able to enter the Bethlehem Steel Key Highway Shipyard in Baltimore for long-overdue repairs, maintenance, and conversion to oil burning. When she returned to service, the plan was to keep the recently renovated *Meteor* despite her age and dispose of the *City of Norfolk*, according to Patrick Parker.

"We were going to do away with her in 1944 but the government said no, you're going to rebuild the *Norfolk* because we're going to take the *Meteor* back," Parker recalled. The work included a new steel freight deck and other new wooden decks, as well as conversion to oil burning. The work on both ships took many months and cost close to $500,000. Those two old boats might have been earmarked for scrapping in 1942 but they certainly showed their mettle in those trying times.[11]

The *Meteor* ended her Old Bay Line service in mid-October 1944 and was then assigned to operate on the Potomac River with the Norfolk and Washington Steamboat Company's *District of Columbia*. She had been running alone since the *Northland* and *Southland* were requisitioned in 1942. For some reason, however, the *Meteor* was not very popular on the Washington run and was returned to the government in April 1946, leaving the *District of Columbia* to once again hold down the service by herself. The *Meteor* was scrapped in New Jersey in 1948.

The clouds of war finally parted and thousands of troops headed home. But many things were uncertain as peace returned, including the future of the Old Bay Line, and the two old and gallant steamboats that had been scheduled for retirement years before. What would the future hold for them?

The Old Bay Line managed to charter the former Long Island Sound night boat *Meteor* to fill in in 1944 while the *City of Norfolk* and *City of Richmond* went to the shipyard for much-needed repairs.

12

Picking Up the Pieces After the War

Following her service on the Seine, the *President Warfield* steamed across the English Channel to Plymouth to await whatever the future held for her. She had already performed yeoman service in several different areas, but there would be no more military assignments in Europe for her—she had done what she came to Europe to do and now she was going home. She and several other vessels formed up in convoy and headed out to sea from Plymouth on July 8, 1945, bound for Norfolk. While the rigors of war duty were now behind her, she still had one more challenge ahead of her—the stormy North Atlantic.

Heavy weather closed in shortly after leaving England, but nothing like the fury the sea hurled at the little fleet after the *Warfield* had stopped for refueling in the Azores. There were 20-foot seas and green water that reached the unprotected windows of the gallery deck, and she rolled and pitched constantly in the heavy seas, recalled Quartermaster Roland Scott.

"It was a real chore trying to keep her bow into the wind," Scott said. "When she rolled, she tended to hang there. I estimate conditions were like that for about a day and a half. We stood some long watches."

Due to the refueling stop and the heavy weather forcing the convoy to dramatically cut speed, the voyage home was a long one, and it was not until the morning of July 25 that the *President Warfield* passed through the Virginia capes and was back in familiar waters. She tied up at the Norfolk Naval Base where the process of decommissioning began. Her naval career was at an end.

Scott had been part of the *Warfield*'s crew for some time and he and some of the other crew members had grown attached to her. "This ship played an important part in my younger life and I know it will for the rest of my time," Scott said, years later.[1]

At the end of World War II, the Old Bay Line was still in business—something that could not be said for many other East Coast companies that had operated passenger and freight steamers before the war.

Companies like the Merchants and Miners Transportation Company, which operated oceangoing steamers up and down the coast, and the Colonial Line, which operated on Long Island Sound, were forced to relinquish their entire fleets for war service. By the time hostilities ended, most of their ships had been lost to enemy action, permanent acquisition by the government, or had been greatly altered and were so run down by war service that their restoration was unfeasible.

While the Old Bay Line was still busier than ever, its situation was far from ideal. It had only two ships, and in the overnight steamship business, it was always desirable to have at least three so there would be one available should one of the regular steamers have to be taken out of service. The *City of Norfolk* and *City of Richmond* were well over thirty years old. One account after the war stated that the *Norfolk* "does not carry her years lightly and it is difficult to get her to better than 16.5 miles an hour."[2]

No sooner had the *Warfield* arrived in Norfolk than top Old Bay Line officials went to visit her. What they saw dismayed them. Although less than twenty years old, the *Warfield* had aged before her time. She was banged up and bruised and was plagued with, among other things, a wooden superstructure that shifted in high seas because of all the strain it had endured during the war years from large numbers of troops.

Although the government eventually reimbursed the company (not until 1949) for the four ships it had taken in 1942, the Old Bay Line decided not to take the former flagship back because of the enormous cost of restoring her for bay service. The *City of Norfolk* and *City of Richmond* would have to continue their hard work alone. Within a short time after her decommissioning, the *President Warfield* was taken to the James River Reserve Fleet to await her fate—a fate that no one could have ever imagined.

Another problem facing the Bay Line was that of suitable docks. As early as 1944, the company was faced with the prospect of losing its docks along Light Street in Baltimore, its home for the past forty-four years. Mayor Theodore R. McKeldin expressed concern over the decrepit condition of many of the wharves along Light Street once used by steamboat companies, many of them vacant. It was an issue that would not be resolved for another five years.[3]

Despite depleted fleets—four boats taken from the Old Bay Line, two from the struggling Norfolk and Washington Steamboat Company, and one from the Pennsylvania Railroad route across the mouth of the Bay—Hampton Roads was a mecca of sorts in 1945 of steamboat operations. Nowhere was this more evident than at the dock at Old Point Comfort, which literally bustled with steamboat activity for a few years after the war.

On any given morning, the Old Bay Line steamer from Baltimore arrived around 5:30 with freight and passengers. Once she departed for Norfolk, the *District of Columbia* of the N&W Line was next to tie up at the government-owned dock at 6:30 a.m. Although the Pennsylvania Railroad's veteran steamer *Elisha Lee* on her morning voyage from Cape Charles to Norfolk did not stop at Old Point, she passed close by. Around 9 a.m. the PRR's other Cape Charles–Norfolk steamer, the *Maryland*, made a stop there before going on to Norfolk. Two hours later, the *Elisha Lee*, on her way back to Cape Charles, did dock at Old Point, to be followed around 2 p.m. by the *Maryland* on her return trip. It was the *Elisha Lee* again shortly before 5:30 p.m., followed by the northbound *District of Columbia* at 7 p.m. and either the *City of Norfolk* or *City of Richmond* headed for Baltimore at 7:30 p.m.[4]

The *City of Richmond* made maritime history early in 1946 by becoming the first commercial passenger vessel in the entire American merchant marine to receive radar, receiving a unit that was built in Baltimore by the Westinghouse Corporation that had a range of up to 32 miles. It was originally intended for installation on United States Lines' passenger liner *America*, but she was still undergoing reconditioning from war duty and was not ready to receive it. So, a very modern-looking radar device was installed on the roof of the steamboat's pilothouse and the system went into service on the *City of Richmond*'s southbound trip to Norfolk on the night of March 18, 1946. Captain Samuel B. Chapman, her master, called radar the most valuable navigational aid he had seen since he started steamboating in 1913.

In the postwar years, the Old Bay Line advertised not only in regional newspapers, but as far away as New York where advertisements regularly appeared in papers such as *The New York Times* and *The Herald Tribune*, urging motorists to take the steamer and save nearly 200 miles of driving to Florida by putting their cars on the ships. The advertisements also promoted the historic area around Colonial Williamsburg and Jamestown and package tours by steamer.

It would appear that after a year in the reserve fleet that the *President Warfield*'s days were numbered, but not so. Reports about the vessel's future had been circulating for some time, reports that variously had her being scrapped or sold for use on Chinese rivers. The Maritime Commission sold her to the Potomac Shipwrecking Company for $8,028, which, in turn, sold her for $40,000 to a New York firm called the Weston Trading Company.

That firm turned out to be a front for the Palestine underground organization Haganah, which was gathering American ships and volunteer American crews to clandestinely transport wartime displaced Jews from Europe to a new home in Palestine, which was administered by Britain. The *Warfield* became a Haganah blockade runner and crossed the Atlantic again in February 1947, eventually reaching the port of Sète, France, where she took aboard a staggering 4,500 Jewish refugees and headed east into the Mediterranean. A Royal Navy task force of a cruiser and three destroyers followed in her wake.[5]

Early on the morning of July 17, as she prepared to make a run to the beaches to land her passengers, two destroyers closed on either side of the steamer trying to get her to stop and struck her, their bows tearing open large sections of the wooden superstructure. Fortunately, the steel hull was not breached. At that point, the steamer's new name boards were revealed showing her new name—*Haganah Ship Exodus 1947*.

The *City of Richmond* in Baltimore harbor in March 1946 when she became the first U.S. merchant ship to be fitted with radar. The large white object on the wheelhouse roof housed the radar screen.

The *President Warfield* was laid up in the James River Reserve Fleet for a year following her war service while rumors circulated that she might again cross the Atlantic. (*U.S. Naval History and Heritage Command, #NH85397*)

The *President Warfield*, renamed *Exodus 1947*, arrives in the port of Haifa, Israel, with 4,500 Jewish refugees following an offshore altercation with British warships that left her damaged. (*Courtesy of the Central Zionist Archives, Jerusalem*)

The damage done to the steamer's superstructure is evident as she eases up to the dock. Amazingly, there were few fatalities during the encounter. (*Courtesy of the Central Zionist Archives, Jerusalem*)

After lying abandoned in Haifa harbor for several years, the *Exodus 1947* was destroyed by fire on August 26, 1952 (*A. Spencer Marsellis* collection)

Royal Marines boarded the steamer and a melee broke out on her decks—the British being pelted by cans of food and potatoes thrown by the refugees. Before long, the British were in control and she was taken into Haifa, Israel, where her passengers were unloaded and put on British ships that took them back to their points of origin. Over time, the *Exodus* became a symbol of the efforts to create the nation of Israel, which became a reality on May 14, 1948. Meanwhile, the battered *Exodus* remained tied up out of the way in Haifa harbor, her sailing days finally over. For an unmatched account of the *Warfield*'s incredible career, David C. Holly's *Exodus 1947* is highly recommended.

The year 1948 saw the end of the long careers of the former Old Bay Line steamers *Florida* and *Alabama* far from home waters. After a west coast career as the ferry *Calistoga*, the *Florida* was used by the navy as an auxiliary at the Mare Island Naval Base in Vallejo, California, during the war and was then scrapped in San Francisco. The *Alabama* had seen service on Puget Sound, and government work in the Pacific Northwest as an accommodation ship and was likewise scrapped in 1948.

On November 1, 1948, there was a collision between the N&W Line's *District of Columbia* and the tanker *Georgia* in fogbound Hampton Roads that damaged the steamer so badly that the company decided to go out of business, clearing the way for the Old Bay Line to buy her and once again have a three-ship fleet. The collision and the vessel's sale are covered in more detail in the chapter entitled *What Might Have Been*. The steamer underwent extensive repairs and resumed sailings on her old route on May 5, 1949.

Her addition to the fleet gave the line some much needed flexibility because she could spell the Baltimore–Norfolk boats whenever they had to be taken out of service. Although she was newer than the other two, she had a small freight capacity and that is probably one of the reasons she did not regularly operate on the Baltimore–Norfolk route where freight was the real moneymaker for the line. Her addition to the fleet also allowed the company to better accommodate tour groups visiting the nation's capital and the historic area around Williamsburg.

The *District of Columbia* makes a fine sight as she departs from Old Point Comfort in the 1950s.

The *District of Columbia* initially operated year-round between Washington and Norfolk for the Old Bay Line, but it was later decided to run her only between April and September and lay her up in Norfolk during the winter months when passenger travel always dropped off. Later, she spent her winters at the Old Bay Line piers in Baltimore.

On December 2, 1949, the Old Bay Line's venerable terminal in Baltimore at Pier Ten, Light Street, was hit by a six-alarm fire that damaged the roof and second floor. It was the latest in a series of fires over the decades, and it is amazing that the bulk of the company's records survived, although a number of important documents were lost to flames over the years.

The city of Baltimore finally announced plans in 1950 to demolish the decaying wooden steamboat piers along Light Street and replace them with a waterfront park. The Old Bay Line refused to leave until a suitable new terminal could be found and it finally arranged with the city to lease Pier Three, Pratt Street, one-time home to the Merchants and Miners Transportation Company. The Bay Line began using the pier in December 1950 and it would be its home for the rest of the line's existence.

On August 25, 1952, the *Exodus 1947* (ex-*President Warfield*) burned at Haifa, Israel, where she had been laid up since her epic voyage. The cause of the fire was never determined and the steel hull was towed away and left to deteriorate in the shallows. In 1963 and 1964, efforts were made to refloat her for salvage but were unsuccessful. There was another salvage effort in 1974; this time, the hull was successfully refloated and was being towed to a nearby river when she sank again for the last time. Portions of the hulk remained visible until the Port of Haifa built a new container terminal about 2005 over the spot where she lay. In 2017, to mark the seventieth anniversary of the *Exodus'* voyage, a memorial was unveiled in the Haifa Cruise Ship Terminal.[6]

November 1954 brought with it for the first time the specter of the Old Bay Line losing its dock at Old Point Comfort. The pier, located on the grounds of the Army's Fort Monroe, was owned by the federal government, which said it was considering

Despite their age, the *City of Norfolk* and *City of Richmond* were kept in top condition and continued to offer the service for which the Bay Line was famous. Here the *City of Norfolk* steams out of Baltimore harbor in the 1950s.

Above left: The two veteran steamers were famous for the elegance of their Edwardian interiors. The main staircase on the *City of Richmond* had brass facings and wrought iron railings that were a throwback to an earlier era. (*A. Spencer Marsellis* collection)

Above right: At the top of the elegant staircase leading to the dining room was the *City of Norfolk*'s carved builder's nameplate. (*A. Spencer Marsellis collection*)

A portion of a small lounge adjacent to the Smoking Room on the *City of Norfolk*, showing the richly colored paneling. (*A. Spencer Marsellis* collection)

Above left: Captain Samuel Boyd Chapman, seen directing the docking of the *City of Richmond* in Norfolk, was her master from 1936 to 1962. (*Photo by Hans Marx*)

Above right: The master of the *City of Norfolk* was Captain Patrick L. Parker, who took command of the steamer in 1943. A group of passengers watches as he directs her docking in Norfolk. (*Hans Marx photo*)

demolishing the wharf because the government no longer used it and it was costly to maintain. As so many tourists who used the steamers got on and off at Old Point to visit the area's historical sites, and because freight business there was doing well, losing the pier would have had a significant impact on the Old Bay Line. Civic organizations and others in the vicinity urged the army not to close the pier, and talk of its demise gradually faded but did not go away entirely.

On August 12, 1955 the *City of Norfolk* was hit by heavy seas in the lower bay that had been whipped up by Hurricane Connie. A portion of the decking and railings on the steamer's quarter deck were badly damaged off Thimble Shoals, a rough place even in calm weather. She was able to continue her voyage, and no one was injured.[7]

13

What Might Have Been

Anyone reading the annual reports of the Old Bay Line from 1946 onward would learn quickly that replacement tonnage was a top priority, whether it be brand new vessels or converted existing ones. New ships were, of course, preferred but the line was open to all options because it was abundantly clear that the *City of Richmond* and *City of Norfolk* could not go on indefinitely.

The first intriguing possibility manifested itself in a brief dispatch that appeared in *Marine News* in May 1946, which stated, "Baltimore Steam Packet Co. Expected to Let Contracts for Three Ships." The two-sentence dispatch said it was understood that plans had been prepared "for the construction of new vessels to replace the three ships *President Warfield*, *State of Maryland* and *State of Virginia*." No mention was made of the *Yorktown*, which had also been requisitioned. Of the several ship replacement possibilities considered in the postwar years, this was the only mention of three new vessels. However, that apparently was all that was ever heard of such of a plan.[1]

An ambitious plan was then developed proposing the acquisition of two Maritime Commission AKA-Class attack cargo carriers built during the war and their conversion to overnight passenger and freight steamers. The two vessels identified for that purpose were the *Scania* and *Mellena*, built in 1944 and 1945 respectively, by the Kaiser-Walsh Company. They were 426 feet in length with a beam of 58 feet, a draft of 15.5 feet, and a speed of 17 knots.

At the company's request, designers at Bethlehem Steel's Sparrows Point shipyard went to work creating plans and specifications for them. "We put in a lot of work on them," said Bethlehem Naval Architect Charles D. Schaub, who personally prepared drawings of the ships, which are dated May 1, 1947. In an interview with the author, he said the designers had to take into account the maneuverability of the much larger ships in Baltimore's confined inner harbor since the smaller *City of Norfolk* and *City of Richmond* already used tugs for undocking. Stability tests were carried out, Schaub said, and the plans were approved by the American Bureau of Shipping.[2] In addition to the plans, several artists' renderings provided a tantalizing look at what the converted vessels would have looked like.

The images showed a single-funnel vessel of contemporary design with six decks, a pearl gray hull with white superstructure and capable of carrying 723 passengers in

An artist's rendering of what a surplus AKA-Class attack cargo carrier would have looked like converted into an Old Bay Line ship.

242 staterooms, 147 of which would have been outside, many with tubs and showers. Most of the rooms would have accommodated three passengers. The ships would have been built of welded lightweight fire-resistant materials. A description prepared by the shipyard stated that decorations would be simple, modern designs, with a minimum of decorative trim. There was, however, no mention of air-conditioning among the amenities.

There would have been considerably more room for cargo than on the old steamers. The ships would have had space for 1,620 tons of general cargo, 100 tons of refrigerated cargo, and room for many more passengers' cars. More and more passengers wanted to bring their cars, but there was limited space for them on the freight decks of the existing bay liners.

In a November 4, 1947 statement, Passenger Traffic Manager Raymond L. Jones described the ships as still being in the dream stage and said that even if they were ordered immediately, it would probably be a year before they could enter service. The estimated cost, he said, would be considerably more than $1 million each. That, however, seems to have been a conservative estimate in light of the much higher amounts shipyards were quoting.

However, nothing further was heard about the plan, possibly because the company knew that it could not yet consider new ships since it had not received government compensation for the four steamers requisitioned in 1942. The compensation issue would not be settled until 1949. Although the question of more modern tonnage remained unresolved for the time being, the Old Bay Line did succeed in adding a much-needed third vessel to its fleet, after the Norfolk and Washington Steamboat Company's *District of Columbia* was badly damaged in a collision.

On the foggy morning of October 31, 1948, the southbound steamer had completed her call at Old Point Comfort and cast off for the last leg of the trip into Norfolk. The steamer, which did not have radar, was making about 8 miles an hour when the anchored tanker *Texaco Georgia* loomed up out of the fog dead ahead. Captain Edward H. Eaton

A portion of the dining room that would have been on the converted surplus wartime AKA vessel.

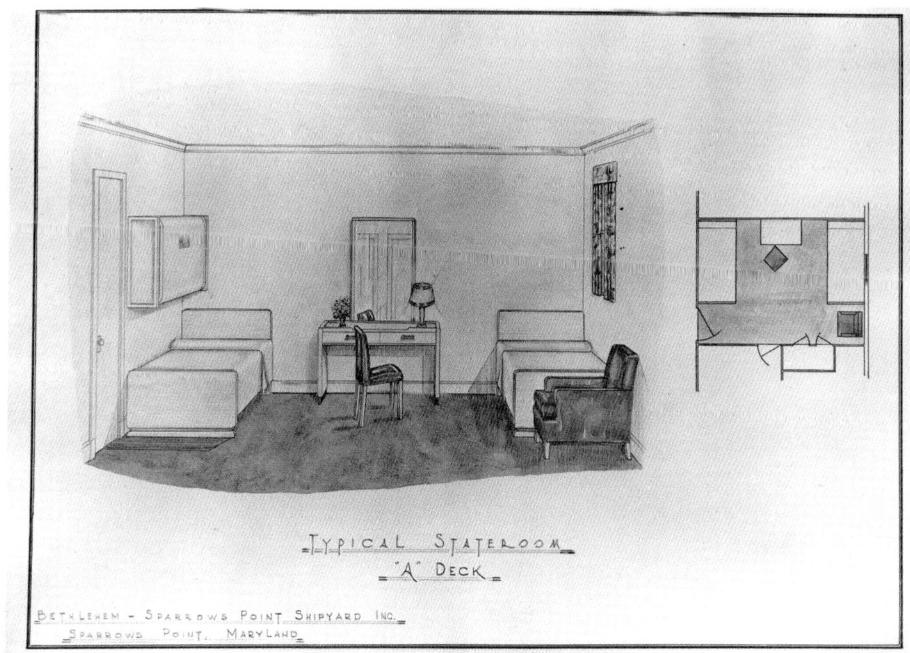

The proposed stateroom accommodations on the converted vessel bear a strong resemblance to those on American deep-sea passenger liners of the period.

took evasive action, but she was too close. The tanker's bow raked the starboard side of the *District of Columbia* and ripped 75 feet of the wooden superstructure wide open from just forward of the funnel to the middle lifeboat toward the stern and from the main deck to the gallery deck. A woman still asleep in her cabin was killed and three other people in their staterooms were hurt. Fortunately, most of the other fifty passengers were either at breakfast in the dining room or on deck at the time. Eaton quickly ran the steamer aground on nearby Hampton Bar because he did not then know the extent of the damage. Once it was determined that she was in no danger of sinking, the passengers were removed by a navy tug and she was moved to her dock in Norfolk.[3]

There was no question what the collision meant for her owners. Business was declining because with only a single steamer daily service could not be offered. "We couldn't make it on an every-other-day basis because you just can't hire people [such as dockworkers] to work one day and not the next. The overhead was too great," Eaton said many years later. He said the company was preparing to shut down even before the collision. "The decision was made that 1948 would be the last year and we all knew it."[4] The collision simply hastened that decision.

The Old Bay Line soon announced that it had bought the steamer and would repair her and resume service between Washington and Norfolk on the same alternate-night basis as the N&W. In addition to collision damage repairs, her interior was overhauled, her boilers were converted to oil firing, and radar was installed. Her acquisition finally gave the line much-needed operational flexibility. On May 5, 1949, the refurbished steamer, dressed fore and aft, sounded her whistle and departed from her Seventh Street wharf in Washington to start the Old Bay Line's new Washington–Norfolk division. Initially, she operated year-round on the Potomac, but because traffic was significantly lighter in winter, it was decided to run her only from the beginning of April to the end of September. She was laid up for the winter at the company's dock in Norfolk.

While the addition of a third steamer was a positive development, it did not address the need for more modern floating equipment. However, 1949 also saw the line finally receive compensation from the federal government for the *President Warfield*, *State of Maryland*, *State of Virginia*, and *Yorktown*—a total of $3,276,082 after taxes and fees.

The Old Bay Line then announced new plans to buy two surplus U.S. Navy landing ship dock vessels (LSDs) for conversion to overnight passenger and freight steamers. According to the company's president, Robert E. Dunn, the converted ships would be able to carry more than 500 passengers in 250 staterooms, 1,000 tons of general cargo, and fifty automobiles and trucks; it would steam at 18 knots. The plan also called for large dining salons, recreation rooms, and cocktail lounges. The two vessels identified by the line's historian Alexander Crosby Brown were the *Highway* (LSD-10) and *Northway* (LSD-11), both launched in 1943 at the Newport News Shipbuilding and Drydock Company yard for transfer to the British flag under Lend-Lease. They had geared turbines, were 457 feet long with a beam of 72 feet, and a maximum draft of 18 feet.[5]

With the addition of the converted LSDs, the company would have had five vessels—the two converted steamers on the Baltimore–Norfolk run and two of the older ones on the Washington–Norfolk run (the *District of Columbia* and either the *City of Richmond* or *City of Norfolk*). The fifth vessel would have been held in reserve. Passenger Traffic Manager R. L. Jones said that the new ships should prove attractive to tourists, many of whom came from out of the area.

The *District of Columbia* of the Norfolk and Washington Steamboat Company was acquired by the Old Bay Line after she was badly damaged in a collision in 1948. She is seen undergoing repairs in Baltimore at which time she was converted to oil firing. (*Photo by A. Leigh Sanders*)

Following repairs, the Old Bay Line put the *District of Columbia* back onto her old run between Washington and Norfolk in May 1949. She is about to depart from the Seventh Street Wharf in Washington.

Left: The interior decoration of the *District of Columbia* included a staircase and mirror at the top. It was said that the mirrors were intended to make the area look larger. (*Photo by Edward O. Clark*)

Below: The Gallery Deck of the *District of Columbia* looking forward. Her interior decoration was somewhat restrained compared with her older running mates. (*Photo by Edward O. Clark*)

"Those LSDs would have made beautiful ships on the bay, no doubt about that, but they were too big and it would have been tough to squeeze them into the slips," said *City of Norfolk* Captain Patrick L. Parker many years later.[6] The government was asking $550,000 for the pair, but the cost of rebuilding them for overnight service on the bay was estimated at $8 million by Bethlehem Steel. It was simply more than the company could afford, and the plans had to be dropped again.

Before long, yet another possibility appeared. In November 1949, Bethlehem Steel drew up plans for a pair of vessels unlike any the Old Bay Line had operated before. Roger L. Gintling, chief naval architect at the Sparrows Point shipyard remarked the following in an interview years later:

> We prepared plans for two identical ships to be built brand new from the keel up ... The Bay Line would have run them on the Chesapeake during the summer and down to Florida during the winter. They would have been miniature ocean liners with a stern loading door so they could carry trucks and other large cargoes.[7]

Their profile was similar to that of the proposed AKA conversions but with no sheer and a squared-off stern to accommodate the big loading door. Slightly shorter than the AKAs, they would have had 217 staterooms and could have carried nearly 2,000 tons of cargo, according to Gintling.

Interestingly, there are two variations of the plan—one for a ship with four passenger decks and another showing a vessel with three passenger decks. Although there is no surviving documentation concerning estimated cost, it may have been that the shipyard was giving the Old Bay Line two options from which to choose to keep the cost down. As it turned out both new build versions proved too expensive and the company was obliged to once again drop the project.

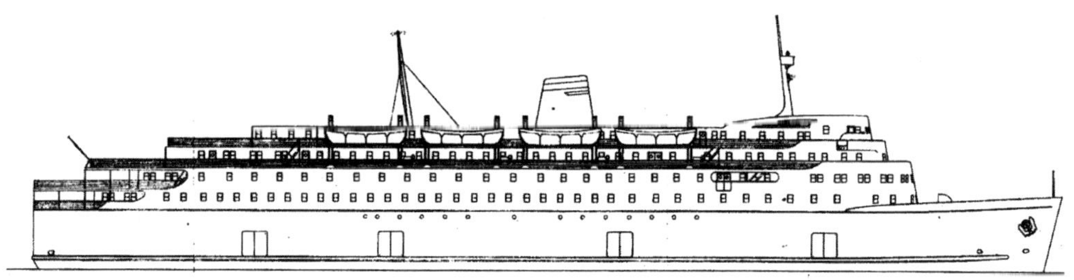

Bethlehem Steel also drew up plans for a new steamer built from the keel up. This is the four-deck version; there was also a three-deck plan as an alternative.

14

The Shadows Lengthen

It could be said that 1955 marked the beginning of the end for the Old Bay Line. There were significant labor issues that year followed in succeeding years by the loss of docks, rising costs of manpower, and the curtailment of service on several levels. There was also always the issue of aging ships, by then operating in their fourth and fifth decades. Despite these various challenges, the management met them head-on with a determination to offer the best service possible. The steamers were well maintained and the on-board service—particularly meals—continued at the same high level, and the company was making a profit.

Passenger service, however, had become a seasonal business used primarily by tourists and vacationers in the warm months. The Old Bay Line eagerly cultivated the tourist trade, especially the various school groups that came from long distances to ride the steamers to and from historic destinations. On many trips, the school groups practically took over a steamer, which to the youngsters, was as much an attraction as destinations like Williamsburg, Jamestown, and Washington, D.C. That business became so lucrative that for a time it required all three steamers on the Baltimore–Norfolk run.

Freight was what really generated revenue year-round. The steamers could carry freight at cheaper rates than many other forms of transportation and the line was an important component of its railroad owners since it gave them access to the Baltimore market even though their rails did not reach the city. As a result, the steamers often sailed with full or nearly full loads of freight. However, a dark cloud gathered in the fall of 1955 that had a major impact on the line, especially its freight business.[1]

In September, a dispute arose over possible unionization of Old Bay Line crew members. The Marine Allied Workers of the Seafarers International Union claimed that the company had fired three employees for union organizing even though there was an agreement between the company and the union that an election on the matter would be held. The dispute led to picketing, charges and counter-charges, and disruptions in service that lasted for extended periods.

Pickets went up at Pier Three, Pratt Street in Baltimore on September 17, and that same day, the *City of Richmond* departed early with only freight, leaving passengers on the dock. The same night, the *District of Columbia* left Washington's Seventh Avenue dock

Old Bay Line steamers spent much of their time in darkness during their 180-mile run between Baltimore and Norfolk. The *City of Richmond* is entering a busy Baltimore harbor during the dark pre-dawn hours in the 1950s. (*Photo by Hans Marx*)

The *City of Norfolk* has arrived at Pier Three, Pratt Street, in brilliant early morning sunlight. The lighters and barges are already alongside.

The *City of Richmond* prepares to back into the Old Bay Line wharf in Norfolk during the 1950s after spending the day calling at marine terminals loading and unloading freight. (*Hans Marx photo*)

without passengers or freight. The *City of Norfolk*'s sailing on the night of September 18 was canceled, also stranding passengers, but the company said that cancellation was because of an approaching hurricane. On September 23, the union filed charges of unfair labor practices against the Old Bay Line with the National Labor Relations Board. By that time, all three of the line's three steamers had been tied up for several days.

The legal wrangling continued and it was not until October 5 that passenger service was resumed when the *District of Columbia* sailed from Washington with forty passengers but no freight. A company official said at the time that freight service was not yet being resumed because longshoremen and tugboat crews were honoring the picket lines. On October 10, despite continued picketing, passenger operations between Baltimore and Norfolk resumed but there was still no freight. Bulk freight, which was the company's real bread and butter, was being prevented by union sympathizers from reaching the piers by lighter. This prompted some of the Bay Line's long-term freight clients to look elsewhere for shipping their goods.

Gradually, freight handlers began crossing the picket lines, and on November 9, the company announced that operations were back to normal, but the Marine Allied Workers leadership insisted its strike was still on and the picketing continued. The dispute went on for several more months until the unions agreed to end picketing at the line's terminals. The end result was that the Bay Line's employees did not join the unions, but the damage had been done. Many of those shippers who had gone elsewhere did not return and at the end of 1955, the company reported a net operating deficit of $68,000 for the year, blaming the loss on the year's labor difficulties.[2]

There was a close call for the *City of Richmond* and the *District of Columbia* while they were docked in Norfolk on April 11, 1956, when the nearby former Merchants and Miners Transportation Company pier caught fire during a severe northeast gale, threatening the Old Bay Line pier next door. The two steamers were moved and anchored in the Elizabeth River until the fire was out and the storm abated the next day, allowing them to depart for Baltimore and Washington.

The future of the government dock at Old Point Comfort came up again in 1956. Municipal leaders from Newport News, Hampton, and Warwick, Virginia, tried to convince the army not to close the dock, saying it was important to their communities. The closure had tentatively been set for June 30, 1956. The Old Bay Line reportedly was interested in buying the wharf because of its importance to the company's freight business.

At the same time, company advertisements enticed travelers to take the steamers to Old Point for the nearby 1957 Jamestown Tercentennial Festival. "Travel as John Smith Did—Take the Boat—You'll Enjoy Your Trip More," the advertisements declared. The army, meanwhile, did not go ahead with its plans to close the Old Point wharf.[3]

The Washington–Norfolk service was suspended as usual for the winter on October 30, 1957, and the *District of Columbia* shifted to the Baltimore–Norfolk run where she filled in while the *City of Norfolk* and *City of Richmond* underwent their regular Coast Guard inspections. Considerable work was required on both vessels and it was not until early February that they were both back on their regular runs.

While the *District* was filling in for the regular boats, the Old Bay Line announced on December 17 that it had cancelled its lease on the Seventh Street dock in Washington, also owned by the government, because part of it was condemned and had been roped off. The company felt it could not use the pier under those conditions. The U.S. Army Corps of Engineers, however, insisted that the portion of the pier where the steamer docked was in usable condition. In his column, *Washington Post* Travel Editor Alexander Henderson mourned the loss of the service:

> It's one thing to say that there is sufficient reason for this, but quite another to make it rest well with the thousands of men, women, and children who have steamed down the river and Bay aboard the boat and its predecessors for the past sixty-seven years.[4]

Although the Old Bay Line said that service had been temporarily discontinued, the *District of Columbia* never again ran on the Potomac River.

On January 7, 1958, the line announced that it was suspending some weekend sailings, the first time in its long history that it did so. It said the move was made to provide more time for overhauling the *City of Norfolk* and *City of Richmond* and that the suspension would last only a few weeks. However, it was also reported that the suspension was caused by the double time longshoremen were demanding for Saturday and Sunday work. The weekend sailings resumed on March 22, 1958, but were then suspended each winter through 1962.

At about the same time, the company decided to add the *District of Columbia* to the Baltimore–Norfolk route to help handle the large groups of school children that made tours of the historic sites of Williamsburg, Jamestown, and Yorktown. That made three steamers in regular operation between Baltimore and Hampton Roads for the first time since before World War II.

Old Bay Line steamers called at Old Point Comfort for well over 100 years. A large crowd of passengers waits on the wharf as the *City of Norfolk* comes alongside. (*Photo by Hans Marx*)

Passengers board the *City of Norfolk* at Old Point Comfort in the 1950s. The Bay Line's last call at the Old Point wharf was on December 31, 1959. (*Photo by Hans Marx*)

Above left: During the 1950s, the Old Bay Line carried hundreds of school children from all over the country on their spring trips to historic Tidewater, Virginia. For many children, riding the steamboat was an adventure of its own.

Above right: So many student trips were booked on the Old Bay Line that in the spring of 1958, all three steamers were needed to handle the large crowds. The *District of Columbia* (left) and the *City of Richmond* sailed together and are about to leave Norfolk for Baltimore. (*Photo by Hans Marx*)

The *District* was paired with the *City of Richmond* and both would leave Baltimore at 6:30 p.m. with the *District* pulling out first and the *Richmond* following soon after. The *District* docked at Old Point Comfort the next morning to disembark the children, while the *Richmond* steamed straight through to Norfolk. For the northbound trip, the *Richmond* left her Norfolk dock at 6:30 p.m. with the *District* following a short time later, and both stopped at Old Point. They left at 7:30 p.m. with the *Richmond* leading the way to Baltimore so she could be first into the dock the next morning. The *City of Norfolk* sailed alone on alternate days.

The lucrative school tours continued through mid-May, and the Bay Line hoped to keep the *District* on the run with the *Richmond* in an effort to attract more passengers traveling with their cars. However, before long, it was back to a single boat in each direction.[5] The pairing of the two steamers was not repeated after 1958.

Also, in the spring of 1958, the company's president, Robert E. Dunn, sent a letter to the Norfolk Chamber of Commerce in which he stated that high labor costs created by the government subsidization of deep-sea shipping operators made it impossible for coastwise shipping to be operated profitably even though there was ample business. Domestic shipping was not eligible for any subsidies. Dunn credited the Bay Line's railroad owners and its loyal employees for its continued operation.

In August of that year, Dunn presented a report to company officials in which he minced no words about its fleet and its financial situation in general:

> The continued use of these obsolete vessels, which had been scheduled for scrapping at the time of the consolidation [the 1941 merger] has caused and is causing a substantial loss of gross revenue, with resultant high overhead in relation to volume; also, excessive maintenance cost; inability to secure and hold passenger and freight business due to inferior and limited accommodations.

He noted that in the ten years ending with 1953 the line had "continuous increases in its freight revenue and generally in its total revenue, and, all things considered, earned a satisfactory income." Yet he also pointed out that operating expenses during the same period rose annually and that "the Bay Line began to experience decreases in its revenue," but could not cut expenses.

Dunn also once again pointed out that the Bay Line did not qualify for government subsidies because it operated solely in domestic waters while deep-sea American-flag vessels did receive subsidies. The lack of a subsidy—coupled with increasing labor costs, not only in ship operation, but in shipbuilding, towing, and other related operations—was proving excessive for the Bay Line, according to Dunn.

On the subject of replacement vessels, he stated that the company had conducted many exhaustive studies of the possibility of building new ships or converting existing ones, both for passenger and freight service or for freight only. The most recent quotation on the cost of newly constructed ships was made on January 4, 1955, by the Bethlehem Steel Company, Dunn said. The cost for one passenger ship with a shaft horsepower of 6,000 would have been $7,505,800 and $8,320,400 for a vessel with 12,000 shaft horsepower. A freight-only vessel of 6,000 shaft horsepower was quoted at $5,989,000 and $6,804,200 for a vessel with 12,000 shaft horsepower. In both instances, it was simply far beyond the company's means.

The report concluded with the ominous statement that government inspection requirements on the *City of Norfolk* and *City of Richmond* were becoming more difficult and expensive and that the upcoming 1960 survey of both vessels could incur considerable expense. Should either or both of the vessels be denied certification, "it would be most difficult, if not impossible to recover," Dunn wrote.[6]

One is tempted to wonder if the Bay Line management ever had any second thoughts about not taking the *President Warfield* back after the war. True, she had been run hard during the war, but she was considerably younger than the *City of Norfolk* and *City of Richmond* and might not have had some of the expensive maintenance problems that plagued the older boats had she been renovated.

The company announced in October 1958 that it was cutting back on the crews of both steamers during the winter months as an economic move. Passenger traffic usually dropped off considerably during the colder months, meaning fewer stewards and attendants were needed during that period. As a result of the trimmed-down crews, the number of passengers the steamers could carry was reduced. The *City of Norfolk* was limited to forty passengers and the *City of Richmond* was limited to twenty-four.

During this period, the Old Bay Line was trying to negotiate a new lease on the Old Point Comfort dock even though the army still seemed determined to close it. The army said it could not afford to maintain the dock, which it said had been damaged during recent severe storms. One proposal that was briefly floated was for the city of Hampton to buy the pier and lease it to the line, but that idea never progressed any further.

Finally, in November 1959, the army made it official—the wharf would be shut down in January 1960 after 160 years of operation. The *City of Richmond* made the last northbound stop on December 30, 1959, and the *City of Norfolk* the last southbound stop the next morning. Acknowledging that docking at Old Point could be difficult because of wind and tides, Captain Patrick L. Parker of the *City of Norfolk* said he had been prevented from landing there only three times since becoming the steamer's master in 1942. "I'm sad to see it go, but there's not much you can do about it," he said.[7] Although arrangements were made to take school tours from the Norfolk pier to the Williamsburg area by bus and to reroute freight through the Old Dominion Freight Line from Norfolk to the peninsula where Old Point was located, all concerned said it would not be the same.

The 1960s dawned with the company still confronted with the same major issues that had dogged it for years—aging ships and rising costs. There was still sufficient cargo to fill the freight deck in both directions and the ships had near capacity loads of passengers in the warm weather months. From Memorial Day to Labor Day 1960, the two steamers carried about 60,000 passengers and 300,000 tons of freight for the year.[8]

As it turned out, bookings for the annual school tours for 1960 were better than they had been in 1958 and 1959. In the warm weather months, newspaper advertisements promoted all-expense vacation trips to Virginia Beach by way of the steamers. Some advertisements called on prospective travelers to "join the happy hundreds on the Old Bay Line."[9]

There were suggestions that the company should consider reactivating the *District of Columbia* for the same type of houseboat cruises that had been so popular on the *State of Virginia* and the *City of Richmond* in the late 1930s and early 1940s. Passenger Traffic Manager Raymond L. Jones said in the fall of 1961 that due to "changing conditions it would not be profitable for us to undertake same at or during these times."[10]

There were also more labor issues in February 1959 and May 1960. In the first instance, the Seafarers International Union alleged that the company had fired two men and refused to re-hire them because of union activity. In the second instance, the International Longshoremen's Association struck for increased pay but the company said it would have to shut down if the union persisted. Both matters, however, apparently were resolved peacefully.[11]

The winter of 1960–61 was unusually severe, and large areas of the bay were covered with thick ice for an extended period. Early on the morning of February 3, 1961, the *City of Richmond* was making her way slowly toward Baltimore in very heavy ice when she ground to a halt around 5:30 a.m. north of the Chesapeake Bay Bridge near Baltimore Light. There were twelve passengers and forty-three crew aboard. Captain Samuel Boyd Chapman reported that it was 12 degrees outside but that everyone was fine. He said the ice surrounding the ship was up to 15 inches thick.[12]

The Coast Guard Cutter *Conifer* tried for several hours to break the ice around the *City of Richmond* before becoming stuck herself and required the assistance of the icebreaker tug *Carolyn*, which was nearby. Once the *Conifer* was freed, the two vessels worked together and were finally able to break the steamer free of the ice, and the *City of Richmond* slowly made her way to Baltimore, docking eleven hours late. Captain Chapman said it was the longest that he had been icebound since beginning his career in 1913.

On September 6, 1961, the company announced that it was suspending all passenger service during the winter months, the first time it had ever done so. Freight service was to continue on a daily basis, except for weekends. There were many people who felt that this unprecedented action meant that the end was near.

The old meets the new. The 1913-built *City of Richmond* steams past the brand-new tanker *Esso Baltimore*, headed for an open house in Baltimore's inner harbor after her trial runs in the summer of 1960. (*Photo by Hans Marx*)

Jones said the company had a very good summer passenger season in 1961 but passenger numbers dropped off dramatically during the winter and it was no longer economical to maintain a full hotel staff in the off-season. Noting that most of the passengers came from outside of Maryland and Virginia, Jones said the line was already fully booked from mid-March to mid-June 1962.[13]

On the surface all indications pointed to a resumption of passenger service in the spring of 1962. In addition to the heavy advance bookings, the interior passenger spaces of both steamers underwent refurbishment during the winter, and by springtime, the interior woodwork looked almost as good as new.

A new element entered the scene on November 1, 1961, when the competing Norfolk, Baltimore and Carolina Line, a Norfolk-based shipping line, introduced its roll-on roll-off freighters *Maryland Clipper* and *Virginia Clipper* for its Baltimore–Norfolk run. They were surplus U.S. Navy landing ship tanks (LSTs) and were easily converted for commercial service. The NB&C Line had been carrying freight since the mid-1920s with small second-hand freighters. The two new ships were all-steel 300-footers, had bow doors that made loading of roll-on-roll-off freight very easy, and were much more efficient than the freight-handling methods on the Old Bay Line steamers. The new vessels could carry cargo in containers, one of the first shipping companies to adopt what was then a new method of freight transportation. The *Maryland Clipper* and *Virginia Clipper* also required smaller crews.[14]

They operated on a similar daily overnight run between Baltimore and Norfolk called "Trailership Service," which proved to be successful almost immediately. "It was a lucrative business," said the NB&C's founder and president, Leigh G. Hogshire, many years later. "One year during the sixties we did ten million dollars' worth of business."[15] There are some who believe that the appearance of the former LSTs was a contributing factor in the eventual demise of the Old Bay Line, but the top two officials of the NB&C Line did not think so.

"I doubt that we sent the Bay Line over the edge," said former NB&C Line President W. Dwight Hooper. "I think they were knocked off more by their old equipment and lack of modernization."

Company founder Hogshire agreed: "The Bay Line's railroad owners were unwilling to adapt to changing times. They simply didn't want to spend the money. We were

The roll-on-roll-off coastal freighter *Maryland Clipper* and her sister ship *Virginia Clipper* of the Norfolk, Baltimore, and Carolina Line competed with the Old Bay Line for freight business in 1961 and 1962. (*Photo by Harry Jones*)

carrying more freight because we had a larger capacity. They were using up much of their capacity with passengers and their cars," he said. Nevertheless, there was no disputing that NB&C's new freighters were moving freight much more efficiently than the Bay Line and in larger quantities per vessel.[16]

Even as the financial noose tightened, the Old Bay Line continued grappling with the question of ship replacement. One approach called for trying to keep the *City of Richmond* and *City of Norfolk* going until 1964 when the big ferries running across the mouth of Chesapeake Bay would be replaced by the new Chesapeake Bay Bridge–Tunnel and could be purchased at attractive prices. Company officials, however, reluctantly concluded they could not wait that long.

There was a glimmer of hope in early 1962 when two vessels that would have been perfect for the Bay Line's freight service became available for purchase. They were the identical sister ships *New Yorker* and *Floridian* that had been built in 1960 in Baltimore for a coastal container service between New York and Florida that did not succeed.

They were 360 feet long, 52 feet wide, with a draft of 14.5 feet, and could carry about 2,000 tons of cargo each, including containers and automobiles at more than 16 knots. The existing older steamers had a freight capacity of about 600 tons each. There were no passenger accommodations on the two motorships but they had modern air-conditioned quarters for the crew. They were inspected by company officials including President Dunn and Captain Patrick L. Parker, all of whom came away impressed.[17]

"If we had gotten those two ships and had a terminal where you could turn around like a ferryboat, it would have been a gold mine," Parker said.[18]

The Bay Line wanted to buy just one and had the financial resources to do so, but the two ships were being offered for sale only as a pair by the Maritime Administration, something the old company could not afford. One of the vessels, the former *Floridian*, was still afloat as late as 2016 and was being operated as the fish processing ship *Riverine Enterprise* out of Bath, Maine.

After that, things moved quickly. On March 19, 1962, the line announced that it would not resume passenger service in 1962 after all. It said, however, that it hoped to do so in 1963. However, the die was cast. There was nowhere else to turn. The end was at hand.

15

The Last Night Boat

The decision not to resume passenger service in 1962 was made despite heavy advance bookings for that year worth an estimated $600,000. If the company ever issued an explanation for that decision, it has not been located.

"I will miss seeing a lot of friends and also I have to cut my crew down, which is very sad, too." said Captain Samuel B. Chapman of the *City of Richmond*, who appeared surprised at the decision. "Our freight business [has] been very good but the weather [has] been very bad."[1]

A number of steamboat historians and enthusiasts quickly sent letters asking if they could make one final voyage. One stated that he would be willing to sign a waiver for insurance purposes and that "I would need no stateroom as I would want to be up all night." The company's president, Robert E. Dunn, replied, saying he wished he could comply with the requests, but "for reasons which are too numerous to go into detail, I must advise you, as I have others, that it is not practical or proper for us to permit you to make the trip you propose."[2]

Then, less than two weeks later on April 2, top company officials were called to a meeting in Dunn's office. When they heard that there was going to be a meeting, some of those officials thought he was going to announce that the railroad owners had finally given the go-ahead to acquire new ships, Captain Parker said. Instead, Dunn announced that the line was going out of business on April 13—news that sent a shock wave through its workforce.

Dunn said rising deficits were the reason for the shutdown, but it is unclear whether the Bay Line's board of directors or the management of the three railroads that owned the line made the decision. Captain Parker said he believed that the order came from the railroad owners.[3]

The news that the nation's last overnight steamship line was shutting down got widespread news coverage and was even carried in *The New York Times* and *The New York Herald Tribune*. It also generated several editorials, including one in *The* [Newport News] *Daily Press*, which invoked changing times and the recent space flight of astronaut John Glenn:

> It is sad to realize that a nation which so desperately needs Col. John H. Glenn, who traveled 88,000 miles in three hours in a rocket, no longer has need for a master bay

A few days before taking the *City of Richmond* on her final voyage, Captain Samuel Boyd Chapman (at far end of table) hosted a luncheon in her dining room for representatives of the Baltimore maritime community with whom he worked for so long. (*Photo by Hans Marx*)

> pilot such as Captain Samuel Boyd Chapman, Gloucester County native, who has sailed a much greater distance in his 50 years on the bay steamers.[4]

Columnist Louis Azrael in *The* [Baltimore] *News Post* commented on a statement made in the company's 1940 centennial history:

> [The line] embarks on its second hundred years with the certain knowledge that future generations will maintain the illustrious history of the past.... Little, if any knowledge remains certain though. And this "certain knowledge" was based on ignorance of the way the use of autos would increase, and of the growth of air travel.[5]

It did not take long for a flurry of activity to break out aimed at keeping the Old Bay Line running. At both ends of the bay, committees were formed to look into ways of lining up public and private funding to buy at least one of the steamers for continued service. The groups met with port interests to discuss the practicalities of continuing the service without the benefit of railroad ownership to provide much of the freight business. "Getting enough freight at both ends of the line is a concern," said Rolf Williams, a Norfolk shipper.

Early suggestions by committee members called for one steamer, most likely the *District of Columbia*, the newest of the boats, to be used in passenger service six months of the year and operate as a dockside restaurant the remainder of the year. As many of the Old Bay Line's passengers visited Colonial Williamsburg over the years, the Committee for the Continuance of the Old Bay Line even approached the Rockefeller Foundation about financial support in keeping the service going. An official of Colonial Williamsburg, however, responded that the organization could not help.[6]

The author paid a final visit to Captain Chapman and the *City of Richmond* on the night of her second-to-last sailing from Baltimore. Both of us spoke in hushed tones, saddened by what was happening. The author then took a last walk through the dimly lit, deserted corridors and public rooms. Cushions had been removed from many of the chairs and the beds in the staterooms had only bare mattresses, the linen having been stowed for the last time. There was a thin film of dust on the recently refurbished woodwork in the various public spaces that would stay with the steamer to the end.

Yet some things had not changed. There was the unmistakable aroma that one associated with a steamboat—the aroma of antiquity that is difficult to describe—the outside light filtering through the stained-glass skylights, and the brass fronts on the main staircases. One delightful aroma that was missing, however, was that of fine food being prepared in the galley. There was also the quiet—no sounds of passengers making their way through corridors and unlocking their stateroom doors and talking excitedly about their upcoming trip. It was heartbreaking to know that such a wonderful tradition was coming to an end.

As the *City of Richmond* got ready to depart on her last round trip, Captain Chapman said he had been hearing from former passengers asking when passenger service would be restored, and he had to reply to them with the sad news that the end had come.[7]

Even as the committees worked frantically to find a way to keep the steamers going, the clock was ticking down to the last departure from Baltimore on April 12. Right on schedule at 6:30 p.m. that day, the *City of Norfolk* slowly backed out of Pier Three in a driving rainstorm to begin the last round trip of an American night boat. A number of people lined the docks to see her off and her departure was recognized by other boats in the harbor as well as by people in cars. They sounded their whistles and horns in salute to the graceful old steamer as she turned and slowly headed out of the inner harbor. Captain Patrick L. Parker, who said he felt like he was losing his home, returned the salutes with three mournful blasts of the *Norfolk*'s steam whistle.[8]

Above left: The *City of Richmond* as she might have appeared from a passing vessel. Painting by C. Leslie Oursler.

Above right: The *City of Richmond* approaches Pier Three, Pratt Street, at the end of one of her final voyages. (*Photo by Hans Marx*)

The *City of Richmond* arrived back in Baltimore on the morning of Friday, April 13, on her final voyage. This time, the order to the engine room of "Finished with Engines" meant the end. That day, the *City of Norfolk* was in Norfolk making stops at the various freight terminals for the last time. Then it was back to the Old Bay Line pier at the foot of Main Street to prepare for her final run up the bay to Baltimore that night. There was a delay in her departure, and it was almost dark when she slipped her lines one more time and quietly steamed out of Norfolk harbor.

The *City of Norfolk* tied up behind the *Richmond* in Baltimore the next morning, Saturday, April 14 and concluded the Old Bay Line's 122-year history. Before leaving the steamer for the last time, Captain Parker lowered her flag and took it home with him.

More than the Old Bay Line died that April—so did the American night boat as an institution, an institution that went back to the earliest decades of the nineteenth century with large fleets on bays, sounds, and rivers across the United States. "Memories of it will linger well into the space age," wrote columnist John Goodspeed in *The* [Baltimore] *Evening Sun*.[8]

The various committees in Baltimore and Norfolk continued to explore ways to obtain the necessary backing to get at least one of the boats running again, but it was an uphill battle. Perhaps Captain Chapman summed it up best: "I don't think you or I will ever see the Old Bay Line steamers run on Chesapeake Bay again," he wrote from his retirement home after tying his steamer up for the last time. "Stop and think—fifty years is a long time to run a steamboat. People will talk, but steamboats are the thing of the past." He closed his letter with an invitation to come visit that included an intriguing final line, "I could tell you some things I would not want to write." To this day the author regrets that that visit never took place, and that final statement remains an enigma.[9]

It was announced on May 26, 1962, that all three ships had been bought by Benjamin B. Wills, operator of various excursion lines, including the Tolchester Line on Chesapeake Bay. The actual transfer of the vessels had taken place three days earlier with the *City of Richmond* being purchased for $10,000, the *City of Norfolk* for $15,000, and the *District of Columbia* for $25,000.[10] Wills had, for a number of years, operated excursion steamers in Maryland, Virginia, New York, and Massachusetts, and it was to the latter state that one of the Old Bay Line steamers would be going.

Wills said that he was sending the *District of Columbia* to operate as a day excursion steamer named *Provincetown* between Boston and Provincetown on Cape Cod. The steamer was dry docked to make her ready for her voyage north and while in the shipyard a number of her inside staterooms were removed, the freight deck was converted into a dance floor, a bow thruster was added, and she received a fresh coat of paint. Her wooden name boards were simply flipped over and the name *Provincetown* was painted on the other side.

Captain Parker took her to Boston, and she began service on the three-hour run on June 20. However, he left about midway through the season to return to his home in Baltimore. In addition to her excursion runs, she was also used as a spectator ship for the America's Cup Races off Newport, Rhode Island, in September. The *Provincetown* completed her summer season at the end of September and returned to Baltimore for winter layup at Pier Three, Pratt Street.

When he bought the three steamers, Wills did not announce any plans for the *City of Richmond* and *City of Norfolk*, but said he did not plan to scrap them. A maritime

Above left: The *City of Richmond*'s First Officer William Walker makes an entry in the log noting the last passing in the night of two Old Bay Line steamers in mid-Bay. (*Photo by Hans Marx*)

Above right: The *City of Norfolk* makes her final freight stop at the Seaboard Railway dock in Portsmouth, Virginia, on April 13. (*Photo by Hans Marx*)

Above left: The dimly lit Old Bay Line pier recedes in the distance as the *City of Norfolk* quietly glides out of Norfolk harbor for the last time. (*Photo by Hans Marx*)

Above right: On the morning of Saturday, April 14, 1962, the *City of Norfolk* approaches the Chesapeake Bay Bridge for the last time. (*Photo by Hans Marx*)

Above left: A deckhand in the lower left heaves a line ashore as the *City of Norfolk* ties up for good in Baltimore on April 14. The *City of Richmond,* docked ahead, ended her career the morning before. (*Photo by Hans Marx*)

Above right: The *District* was renamed *Provincetown* and was sent to Massachusetts to operate as a day excursion boat between Boston and Provincetown. Here, she is about to get underway from the old Eastern Steamship Company pier in Boston. (*Photo by William H. Ewen, Jr.*)

trade publication carried an advertisement in August 1962 in which both steamers were offered for sale, stating that they would make good floating hotels or quarters for large construction crews. No asking price was included in the advertisement.

Wills apparently reconsidered a short time later and said in September that he expected to resume Baltimore to Norfolk and Washington to Norfolk service with the two veteran steamers in the spring of 1963. The announcement stated that the restored service would be for passengers only and would not be daily. Both steamers were to be taken to Norfolk for refurbishing. Wills' employees reportedly also set up operations in the former Old Bay Line pier in Norfolk.

Meanwhile, the Tourist Committee of the Norfolk Chamber of Commerce commissioned a study in November 1962 to determine whether a renewed Chesapeake Bay service would be profitable. In May 1963, the results of the study were released and showed that such an operation would not be financially self-supporting. After that, there were no more studies and nothing further was heard about the Wills plan for restoring service. It is unclear whether that study was a factor in Wills not going ahead with a resumption of Baltimore–Norfolk service.

He was, however, exploring other options for the old boats, including their possible sale to an undisclosed party in Mexico for use as motels. He was asking $25,000 for each of the steamers in 1963. However, the ships never went anywhere and remained laid up at Pier Three.[11]

The *Provincetown* returned to Boston for another season of excursions on June 17, 1963. She ran through the summer and returned to her familiar dock in Baltimore in early September. It was widely expected that she would return to Boston for the summer of 1964 because Wills had agreed to operate a boat there for one more summer but she

After B. B. Wills bought the Bay Line steamers in May 1962, he indicated he might try to resume service but nothing came of that possibility. Instead, he put the *City of Norfolk* and *City of Richmond* up for sale. The *District of Columbia,* meanwhile, returned to operation, but not on Chesapeake Bay.

never steamed again. The Coast Guard informed Wills in October 1963 that if she were to operate in 1964, a long list of deferred repairs had to be made. With her small amount of open deck space and an interior filled with staterooms, she really was not well-suited for the daytime excursion trade. As a result, all three Old Bay Line steamers languished in layup together at Pier 3 and were joined by *S.S. Potomac*, another veteran excursion steamer also owned by Wills. Incidentally, *S.S.*, which stands for "steam ship," was part of the vessel's official registered name.

At one point in 1964, there was talk along the Baltimore waterfront that one of the steamers might be used as a floating hotel at the New York World's Fair, which was being held that year. No one seems to know where the story originated, but both B. B. Wills and World's Fair officials said there were no plans to use the ships in that capacity. So, the old vessels remained laid up at their Pratt Street pier.

16

Epilogue

The final years for the Old Bay Line's last steamers were ones of dashed hopes and frustration as plan after plan to preserve all three one by one failed to materialize. One plan, however, came close to fruition. In May 1964, the *City of Richmond* was sold for use as a floating hotel, restaurant, and night club at Charlotte Amalie in the Virgin Islands. Plans called for the hurricane deck to be converted to a night club seating 350 people and a band. The dining room was to be refurbished as the restaurant and the staterooms would be renovated and air conditioned to serve as the hotel.

A group of young workers spent much of the summer of 1964 in Baltimore loading hotel and other equipment aboard that would be used in her conversion upon arrival. The author was part of that work crew and was to have made the voyage to the Virgin Islands, but the loading lasted longer than expected and he had to leave the ship to begin college. The workers filled her lower freight holds and the freight deck with equipment to be used in her conversion once she reached Charlotte Amalie. Working below decks on a dead ship in the heat of a Baltimore summer was extremely difficult.

On August 13, 1964, accompanied by a fireboat salute off Fort McHenry, the *City of Richmond* was towed away from Baltimore forever. Then came the news on September 28 that after a delay in Norfolk, the steamer and her tug had been taken into Morehead City, North Carolina, by the Coast Guard Cutter *Chilula* because the tug had broken down offshore. A new tug, the *Carville*, was brought in and the tow resumed on October 3, but then the veteran steamer ran into trouble.[1]

She was off the coast of South Carolina early on the morning of October 5 with seas running high from the remnants of a storm and she started to take on water. The tug sought refuge in Georgetown, South Carolina, but time ran out for the *City of Richmond*. At about 5:25 a.m., moments after the seven men who were riding her went over the side, the steamer rolled to port and what was believed to be air trapped inside blew out part of the wooden starboard side. One of the crewmen said she "busted up like it had exploded" before going under. All seven crewmen were rescued.[2]

She settled upright on the bottom in 49 feet of water about 12 miles off the coast, and about 20 feet of her stack remained above the surface for a short time before being toppled by the heavy seas. Although there was talk of trying to raise her steel hull, nothing came of that idea.

In 1964, the *City of Richmond* was bought for conversion to a hotel, night club, and restaurant in the Virgin Islands. As a fireboat saluted her, she was towed out of Baltimore harbor for the last time. The author, who just happened onto the scene, had to settle for a distant, not very sharp, photo. (*Photo by the author*)

Exactly one week after the *City of Richmond* sank, her longtime master, Captain Samuel Boyd Chapman, died of a heart attack at the age of seventy. A steamboating man for fifty-one years, he had begun his career with the Chesapeake Line and spent most of his service on the *Richmond*. He was her skipper from 1936 to 1962.

In the more than half a century since her loss, the *City of Richmond* has proved to be a popular destination for recreational divers, who have brought up a number of small artifacts from her. Many of them consider her one of the more interesting wrecks along the South Carolina coast.[3]

A few weeks later, it was announced that the *City of Norfolk* was to become a floating hotel and restaurant. Once again, the hopes of area steamboat enthusiasts soared. The new owner said he planned to invest $400,000 in her restoration and hoped to have her in operation in her new role by summer 1965. However, over time, the anticipated financial support did not develop despite the vigorous efforts of those involved. It became apparent that while there was much interest in preserving the old steamer—that interest was more sentimental than financial—and the funding simply did not materialize. Little more was heard of the plan and the steamer remained at her Baltimore dock.

Then in January 1965 came a completely unexpected announcement. A new company named the Chesapeake Bay Line, Inc. had been formed to buy the *Provincetown* from Wills and return her to service as a cruise ship on the bay. She was to be refurbished, renamed *Chesapeake*, and make two and three-day cruises between Washington and Norfolk and Yorktown, Virginia. Plans called for all outside rooms with showers and baths in most rooms, a cocktail lounge, dance hall, recreation deck, and ship's orchestra. The purchase price was $147,815 and the new owners said they planned to spend $40,000 on renovations.

The new company was made up of Baltimore and Washington area business people, including Wills, and was headed by Charles Hoffberger, a respected Baltimore businessman. It developed an attractive logo, and printed colorful brochures and

On October 5, 1964, while being towed off of Georgetown, South Carolina, in rough seas, the *City of Richmond* sank in 49 feet of water and was a total loss. Since then, she has proved to be a popular site for recreational divers.

For a brief time in 1965, it appeared that a new company would be returning the *Provincetown,* to be renamed *Chesapeake,* to service on Chesapeake Bay as a cruise ship, but the proposal came to naught.

reservations began pouring in on the strength of the announcement alone before a single coat of paint could be applied. Hoffberger said that the initial response was amazing, that the ship was booked solid through April, May, and part of June without the benefit of advertising. He said a few reservations had even been received from Europe.[4]

Unfortunately, the Chesapeake Bay Line, Inc., would soon find itself out of business without having carried a single passenger. It turned out that the repairs and refinements required by the Coast Guard to return the vessel to service would cost more than $300,000, and it was simply more than the new company could afford.

A disappointed Hoffberger and his associates had no alternative but to sell her. Before long, negotiations were said to be taking place with several potential buyers interested in converting her into a floating restaurant and hotel. She and the *City of Norfolk* remained tied up in Baltimore, however, and with no maintenance began to deteriorate badly.[5]

Through a series of ship trade-in programs, both steamers eventually became the property of the U.S. Maritime Administration, which offered them for sale in 1966 for non-transportation use. The *City of Norfolk* was the first to go. She was purchased for scrapping in May 1966 by the North American Smelting Company of Fieldsboro, New Jersey. Fortunately, a number of artifacts were saved, including one of the stained-glass domes that once surmounted her Saloon, and has been preserved at the Mariners' Museum in Newport News, Virginia. However, the old steamer did not go quietly. As the scrapping progressed, she was struck by lightning on the night of August 17, 1966, and the ensuing fire consumed what was left of her wooden superstructure, leaving only her steel hull to be broken up.

A few weeks later, it was revealed that the *Provincetown* had been sold for conversion into a floating restaurant. The new owner considered several sites and eventually decided that she should remain in Baltimore where, after restoration, she would be known as The Old Bay Line Inn, located in the renovated Inner Harbor.

But then, on June 4, 1969, a six-alarm fire apparently set by vandals heavily damaged the steamer, burning out large portions of her wooden superstructure and leaving her pilothouse partially collapsed. She was still afloat but presented a pathetic sight with her charred sides and sagging upper works.

Her owner said he hoped he could still go ahead with the restoration plans despite the damage. Eventually, however, the ship was towed to the dead ship anchorage in the Curtis Bay section of Baltimore harbor in mid-1970, joining two former passenger liners awaiting scrapping. It was expected that she would follow them to the scrap heap.[6]

However, on January 13, 1971, the *Provincetown* began slowly taking on water at her anchorage and quietly settled on the bottom a short distance offshore in Curtis Bay. She was submerged up to her saloon deck, and before long, the elements made short work of her wooden superstructure, leaving only the steel funnel and engine casing above water. Over time, they toppled over and disappeared below the surface; to this day, her 300-foot hull still rests on the muddy bottom.

The story finally came to an official end on June 5, 1973, in an office on the fourteenth floor of the Maryland National Bank Building in Baltimore. In that quiet room, five directors of what remained of the Baltimore Steam Packet Company certified to the Maryland Department of Assessments and Taxation that "the corporation has no known creditors" and was "hereby dissolved," officially wrapping up the company's affairs.[7]

While being broken up in 1966, the *City of Norfolk* was struck by lightning, setting off a spectacular blaze. (*Photo by Bill Hensley*)

Above left: In June 1969, the *Provincetown* was badly damaged in a six-alarm fire set by vandals. This view looks forward at what remained of the main staircase. (*Photo by the author*)

Above right: After being towed to the dead ship anchorage on the outskirts of Baltimore harbor to await scrapping, she sank. Within a short time, wind and waves carried away her wooden superstructure. Her remains are still on the bottom today. (*Photo by the author*)

Endnotes

Introduction

1 *The Sun*, March 18, 1840, p. 1.

Chapter 1

1 *The Beacon*, July 31, 1817.
2 *The Sun*, October 30, 1840, p. 1.
3 Scharf, J., *Scharf's Chronicles of Baltimore* (Baltimore, MD. Turnbull Brothers, 1874), pp. 505–506.

Chapter 2

1 *The Sun*, June 28, 1852, p. 1.
2 *Ibid*., February 1, 1859, p. 1.
3 *Ibid*., August 5, 1860, p. 2.
4 Kelley, W., *Baltimore Steamboats in the Civil War* (Baltimore, MD., Maryland Historical Society Magazine, Spring 1942), pp. 42–52.
5 Cornell University Library, *The Official History of the Union and Confederate Navies* (Ithaca, N.Y. collections.library.cornell.edu/moa_new/ofre.html).
6 *The Baltimore Patriot* via *The New York Times*.
7 Naval History and Heritage Command, *Dictionary of American Fighting Ships* (Washington, D.C. hazegray.org/danfs).
8 Sheads, S. and Toomey, D., *Baltimore During the Civil War* (Linthicum, MD., Toomey Books, 1997), p. 62.

Chapter 3

1 Quarstein, J. and Clevenger, J., *Old Point Comfort Resort* (Charleston, SC, The History Press, 2009), pp. 36–37.
2 history.navy.mil/research/histories/ship-histories/danfs.html, *Dictionary of American Fighting Ships* (Washington, D.C.), Naval History Center.
3 *The Sun*, October 24, 1865, p. 4.
4 *New York Times*, December 9, 1866.
5 Brown. A., *Steam Packets on the Chesapeake* (Cambridge, MD., Cornell Maritime Press, 1961), p. 57.
6 Prince, R., *Seaboard Air Line Railroad* (River, Wyo., Indiana University Press, 1966), p. 28.
7 Shomette, D., *Ghost Fleet of Mallows Bay* (Centreville, MD., Tidewater Publishers, 1996), pp. 12–15.
8 *The Sun*, January 20, 1864.

9 *Ibid.*, November 16, 1874.
10 *Ibid.*, April 5, 1876.
11 Holly, D., *Chesapeake Steamboats: Vanished Fleet* (Centreville, MD., Tidewater Publishers. 1994), p. 9.
12 Brown, *op. cit.*, p. 68.

Chapter 4
1 Burgess, R. and Wood, H. G., *Steamboats Out of Baltimore*, (Centreville, MD., Tidewater Publishers, 1968), p. 164.
2 *The Sun*, 15, 1892, p. 8.
3 Correspondence between R. Hoffman and R. Foster (University of Michigan Library), pp. 3–4.
4 *Ibid.*, pp. 7, 20, and 26.
5 *Baltimore American*, July 3, 1896.
6 Brown, A., *Steam Packets on the Chesapeake* (Cambridge, MD., Cornell Maritime Press, 1961), p. 86.
7 *The Sun*, December 10, 1897, p. 5.
8 Brown, *op. cit.*, p. 80.
9 Hall, C. *Baltimore: Its History and Its People, Vol. III (*New York, N.Y. Lewis Historical Publishing Co., 1912), p. 849.
10 *Ibid.*, pp. 134–135.
11 Brown, *op. cit.*, March 11, 1910, p. 14.
12 *International Marine Engineering*, August 1911, p. 318.
13 Old Bay Line advertisement, February 1911.
14 *The Marine Review*, January 1914, p. 11.
15 *Ibid.*, June 24, 1915, p. 20.
16 *Constitution Daily*, December 26, 1918.
17 *The Sun*, May 24, 1919, p. 1.
18 *Ibid.*, p. 13.

Chapter 5
1 Steiner, B., *Men of Mark in Maryland, Vol. III* (B.F. Johnson, Inc., New York, N.Y., 1910), p. 24.
2 *Ibid.*, p. 26.
3 *The Sun*, December 28, 1920, p. 16.
4 Baltimore Steam Packet Company Records, Maryland Historical Society.
5 Information received from Robert H. Hanson.
6 *Commerce and Maritime Record*, July 27, 1922, p. unknown.
7 *Ibid.*, July 27, 1922, p. unknown.
8 Baltimore Steam Packet Company Records, Maryland Historical Society.
9 *Ibid.*
10 *Ibid.*
11 Reeves, C., *Carpe Diem: The 20th Century Pilgrimage of an Imparfit Knight* (Baltimore, MD. Gateway Press, Inc. 1999), pp. 99–101.
12 *The Sun*, October 27, 1927, p. 9.
13 *Interim Report on the Career of the* President Warfield, *The American Neptune*, *Vol. VIII*, *No.* 2, 1948.
14 *Marine Engineering and Shipping Age*, September 1928, pp. 469–475.
15 *Ibid.* p. 476.
16 *The Nautical Gazette*, August 1928, page unknown.
17 Unidentified clipping in author's collection.

Chapter 6
1 *The Sun*, July 24, 1977, p. 261.
2 Ibid. March 6, 1929, p. 24.

3 *The News American*, December 17, 1980.
4 Old Bay Line Advertisement.
5 *Ibid.*
6 *The Sun*, July 30, 1937, p. 1.

Chapter 7

1 Brown, A. *Steam Packets on the Chesapeake* (Cambridge, MD., Cornell Maritime Press, 1961) p. 4.
2 Chesapeake Line Menu, 1932.
3 Old Bay Line Menu, 1935.

Chapter 8

1 Brown, A. *Steam Packets on the Chesapeake* (Cambridge, MD, Cornell Maritime Press, 1961), pp. 58–61.

Chapter 9

1 Patrick L. Parker interview.
2 *Ibid.*
3 *The Sun*, August 26, 1933, p. 3.
4 Parker, *op. cit.*

Chapter 11

1 Estate of Hans Marx.
2 Dill, A., *Chesapeake Corporation: Pioneer Papermaker* (West Point, Virginia, Chesapeake Corporation, 1987), pp. 190–191.
3 John Winter interview.
4 Patrick L. Parker correspondence, April 27, 1974.
5 www.uboat.net
6 Winter interview.
7 German High Command broadcast, September 28, 1942.
8 Holly, D. C., *Exodus 1947* (Boston, Massachusetts, Little Brown and Company 1969), pp. 21–22.
9 Vessel World War II Service Record.
10 American Merchant Marine Museum ship records.
11 *The Sun*, July 31, 1943, p. 5.
12 Patrick L. Parker interview.

Chapter 12

1 Roland Scott interview.
2 Wood, H. G., *A Room with a View* (Flushing, N.Y., *Steamboat Bill*, Steamship Historical Society of America, April 1946), p. 363.
3 *The Sun*, May 20, 1944, p. 12.
4 Wood, *op. cit.*, pp. 326–363.
5 Holly, D. C., *Exodus 1947* (Boston, Massachusetts, Little Brown and Company, 1969) pp. 152–153.
6 *Times of Israel*, July 27, 2017.
7 Lochhead, J., *Chesapeake Bay and South* (Staten Island, N.Y., *Steamboat Bill*, Steamship Historical Society of America, December 1955) p. 92.

Chapter 13

1 *Marine News*, May 1946, p. unknown.
2 Roger Gintling and Charles Schaub interviews, *c.* 1975.
3 *Washington Post* or *Washington Star*, date unknown.

4 Edward H. Eaton interviews, various dates.
5 *The Sun*, March 1, 1949, p. 28.
6 Patrick L. Parker interview.
7 Gintling, *op. cit.*

Chapter 14

1 Burgess, R. and Wood, H.G., *Steamboats Out of Baltimore* (Cambridge, MD. Cornell Maritime Press, 1968), pp. 176–177.
2 Old Bay Line Annual Report for 1955.
3 Unidentified clipping in author's collection.
4 *Washington Post*, December 22, 1957.
5 Lochhead, J., *Chesapeake Bay and South* (Staten Island. N.Y.*Steamboat Bill*, Steamship Historical Society of America), June 1958, p. 43.
6 Dunn, R., *Study of the Baltimore Steam Packet Company*, Baltimore, MD. August 6, 1958. Various pages.
7 *The Daily Press*, January 31, 1959.
8 *The Sun*, November 27, 1960, p. 35.
9 *c.* 1960 newspaper advertisement, author's collection.
10 Correspondence from Raymond L. Jones, May 31, 1961.
11 Miller, M., *End of the Night Boat: Final Years of the Baltimore Steam Packet Company* (U.S. Coast Guard Academy unpublished thesis, Spring 1978).
12 *The News Post*, February 3, 1961.
13 *The Evening Sun*, September 7, 1961, p. 68.
14 *The Virginian Pilot*, July 11, 1961, p. unknown.
15 Shaum, J., *One Man's Shipping Company* (Providence, RI, *Steamboat Bill*, Steamship Historical Society of America), Spring 1998, p. 14.
16 *Ibid.*, p. 18.
17 Miller, *op. cit.*
18 Patrick L. Parker interview.

Chapter 15

1 Correspondence between S. B. Chapman and A. S. Marsellis, March 21, 1962.
2 Correspondence between A. S. Marsellis and Robert E. Dunn March 26–27, 1962.
3 Patrick L. Parker interview.
4 *The Daily Press*, April 8, 1962, p. 2.
5 *The News Post*, April 5, 1962, p. unknown.
6 Ibid. April 10, 1962, p. unknown.
7 *The Sun*, April 13, 1962, p. 46.
8 *The Evening Sun*, April 17, 1962, p. 19.
9 Correspondence with S.B. Chapman, June 19, 1962.
10 U.S. Coast Guard bills of sale for steamers.
11 B. B. Wills correspondence with Robert Rodregues, June 18, 1963.

Chapter 16

1 *The Carteret County News-Times*, September 29, 1964, p. unknown.
2 *Charleston News and Courier*, October 5, 1964, p. unknown.
3 Correspondence with Wendell M. Patton, III, various dates.
4 Cudahy, B., *Twilight on the Bay* (Centreville, MD., Tidewater Publishers, 1998), pp. 169–170.
5 *The Sun*, June 28, 1965, p. 26.
6 *The Evening Sun*, June 5, 1969, p. 34.
7 *Articles of Dissolution, Maryland Department of Assessments and Taxation*, June 5, 1973.

Bibliography

Books

Brown, A., *Steam Packets on the Chesapeake* (Cambridge, MD: Cornell Maritime Press, 1961); *Good Ships of Newport News* (Centreville, MD: Tidewater Publishers, 1976)

Burgess, R., *This Was Chesapeake Bay* (Cambridge, MD: Cornell Maritime Press, 1963); *Chesapeake Circle*: (Cambridge, MD: Tidewater Publishers, 1965)

Burgess, R. and Wood, H. G., *Steamboats Out of Baltimore* (Centreville, MD: Tidewater Publishers, 1968)

Carroll, D., *Men of Mark in Maryland* (Baltimore, MD. B.F. Johnson, Inc. 1907–1912)

Coombe, J., *Gunsmoke Over the Atlantic: First Actions of the Civil War* (New York: Bantam Publishers, 2008)

Cudahy, B., *Twilight on the Bay: The Excursion Boat Empire of B.B. Wills* (Centreville, MD: Tidewater Publishers, 1998)

Dill, A., *Chesapeake: Pioneer Papermaker* (West Point, VA. Chesapeake Corporation, 1968-1987)

Dunbaugh, E., *New England Steamship Company: Long Island Sound Night Boats Of the Twentieth Century* (Gainesville, FL. University Press of Florida/Steamship Historical Society of America.2005); *Night Boat to New England* (Westport, CT: Greenwood Press, 1992); *The Era of the Joy Line* (Westport, CT: Greenwood Press, 1982)

Edwards, B., *The Decoys: A Tale of Three Atlantic Convoys, 1942* (Annapolis, MD: U.S. Naval Institute Press. 2017)

Emmerson, J. C., Jr., *The Steamboat Comes to Norfolk Harbor* (Portsmouth, VA: John C. Emmerson, Jr. 1949)

Fox, W., *Always Good Ships* (Norfolk, VA: The Donning Company, 1986)

Gentile, G., *Shipwrecks of the Chesapeake Bay in Virginia Waters* (Jim Thorpe, PA: Gary Gentile Productions, 2014)

Gibson, C. and Gibson, E., *Over Seas: U.S. Army Maritime Operations 1898 Through the Fall of the Philippines* (Camden, ME: Ensign Press, 2002)

Hall, C., *Baltimore: Its History and Its People in Three Volumes* (New York: Lewis Historical Publishing Company, 1912)

Hilton, G., *The Night Boat* (Berkeley, CA. Howell-North Books, 1968)

Holly, D., *Chesapeake Steamboats Vanished Fleet* (Centreville, MD. Tidewater Publishers, 1994); *Exodus 1947* (New York, NY: Little, Brown and Company.1969)

Jones, H. and Jones, T., *Night Boat on the Potomac* (Providence RI: Steamship Historical Society of America. 1996)

Kelly, J., *Bygone Baltimore* (Norfolk, VA: The Donning Company. 1982)

Lytle, W. and Holdcamper, F., *Merchant Steam Vessels of the United States, 1790–1868* (Staten Island, NY. Steamship Historical Society of America, Inc. 1975)

Mallison, F., *The Civil War on the Outer Banks* (Jefferson, NC. McFarland Publishers. 1997)

Marestier, J., *Memoir of Steamboats of the United States of America* (Mystic, CT: The Marine Historical Association, Inc. 1957)

Mason, A., *History of Steam Navigation to the Eastern Shore of Virginia* (Richmond, VA: The Dietz Press, Inc., 1973)

Mills, E., *Chesapeake Bay in the Civil War* (Centreville, MD. Tidewater Publishers.1996)

Prince, R., *Steam Locomotives and Boats of the Southern Railway System* (Green River, Wyo. Richard E. Prince. 1965); *Seaboard Air Line Railroad Steam Boats, Locomotives, and History* (Bloomington, IN: Indiana University Press. 1966)

Quarstein, J. and Clevenger, J., *Old Point Comfort Resort* (Charleston SC: The History Press. 2009)

Reed, J., *Convoy Maniac—RB-1* (Sussex, England. The Book Guild. 2000)

Reeves, C., *Carpe Diem: The Twentieth Century Pilgrimage of an Imparfit Knight* (Baltimore, MD. Gateway Press, Inc. 1999)

Scharff, J., *The Chronicles of Baltimore* (Baltimore, MD: Turnbull Brothers, 1874); *History of Baltimore City and County.* Philadelphia, PA: Louis H. Everts. 1881.

Sheads, S. and Toomey, D., *Baltimore During the Civil War* (Linthicum, MD: Toomey Books. 1997).

Shomette, D., *Shipwrecks on the Chesapeake* (Centreville, MD: Tidewater Publishers. 1982); *Ghost Fleet of Mallows Bay* (Centreville, MD: Tidewater Publishers. 2009)

Stanton, S., *Steam Vessels of Chesapeake and Delaware Bays and Rivers* (Newport News, VA: The Mariners' Museum. c.1966)

Stieff, F., *Eat, Drink and Be Merry in Maryland* (Baltimore, MD. Johns Hopkins University Press, 1932–1960)

Newspapers

Baltimore American, Baltimore, Maryland
Baltimore Patriot, Baltimore, Maryland
Beacon, Norfolk, Virginia
Carteret County News-Times, Morehead City, North Carolina
Charleston Evening Post, Charleston, South Carolina
Daily Press, Newport News, Virginia
Evening Sun, Baltimore, Maryland
New York Herald Tribune, New York, New York
News and Courier, Charleston, South Carolina
Gazette and Ledger, Norfolk, Virginia
News American, Baltimore, Maryland
News-Post, Baltimore, Maryland
Norfolk Post, Norfolk, Virginia
Sun, Baltimore, Maryland
Trenton Evening News, Trenton, New Jersey
Virginian-Pilot, Norfolk, Virginia
Washington Post, Washington, D.C.
Washington Star, Washington, D.C.
Times of Israel, Jerusalem, Israel

Periodicals

Maryland Historical Magazine, Baltimore, MD
International Marine Engineering, New York, NY
Marine News, New York, NY
The Maritime Reporter and Engineering News
Merchant Vessels of the U.S., Washington, DC
Ships and the Sea, Milwaukee, WIS
Steamboat Bill, Warwick, RI
Travel Weekly, Secaucus, NY

Documents
Advertising materials of the Baltimore Steam Packet Company, Chesapeake Steamship Company, and Chesapeake Bay Line, Inc.
Affidavits of vessels' masters, Convoy RB-1, National Archives of Britain.
Articles of Dissolution, Maryland Department of Assessments and Taxation.
Baltimore Steam Packet Company records, Maryland Historical Society.
Baltimore Steam Packet Company records, Chesapeake Bay Maritime Museum.
Study of the Baltimore Steam Packet Company, Old Bay Line, by Robert E. Dunn.
U.S. Coast Guard documents.
The Papers of Benjamin B. Wills, Calvert Marine Museum.

Web Sites
NavSource Online: The Amphibious Photo Archive (http://shipscribe.com/usnauxIX3/IX167.html)
Ahoy-Mac's Web Log: Naval, Maritime, Australian History and More (ahoy.tk-jk.net)
NOAA Weather History (www.erh.noaa.gov/Hur30s.html)
Newspapers.Com by Ancestry
www.uboat.net

Correspondence
George Bille, American Merchant Marine Museum
Robert H. Burgess, curator of exhibits, The Mariners Museum
Samuel B. Chapman, master, steamer *City of Richmond*
Brian J. Cudahy, maritime author and historian
Raymond S. Edwards, International Underwater Research Corporation
Robert Inglehart, City of Norfolk Corporation
Raymond L. Jones, Old Bay Line passenger traffic manager
Patrick L. Parker, master, steamer *City of Norfolk*
Robert W. Parkinson, maritime historian
Wendell S. Patton III, underwater wreck explorer
R.J. Pelzer, London Facilities, marine insurance firm
Shepard G. Powell, Chesapeake Bay Line, Inc.
Captain G.R. Reynolds, U.S. Coast Guard, Seventh District
Roland Scott, quartermaster, U.S.S. *President Warfield*

Interviews
Edward H. Eaton, master, steamer *District of Columbia*
Roger L. Gintling, chief naval architect, Bethlehem Steel Corporation
Leigh G. Hogshire, chairman, Norfolk, Baltimore and Carolina Line
W. Dwight Hooper, president, Norfolk, Baltimore and Carolina Line
Patrick L. Parker, master, steamer *City of Norfolk*
Charles D. Schaub, naval architect, Bethlehem Steel Corporation
Roland Scott, quartermaster, U.S.S. *President Warfield*
Harry W. Slye, first officer, steamer *District of Columbia*
William John Charles Winter, second radio operator, steamer *Yorktown*

Index

Adelaide (steamer, 1854) 27-30, 31, 32
AKA conversion proposal 122-123
Alabama (steamer, 1837) 20
Alabama (steamer, 1892) 39-42, 46-47, 56, 58, 62, 104
Alcyone (freighter, 1907) 90
Almy, William C. 58, 66-67
Atlanta (steamer, 1897) 43, 47, 51-52
Atlantic Blockading Squadron 30
Atlantic Coast Line 41, 47, 95
Atlantic Steam Packet Company 19-20
Augusta (steamer, 1900) 47, 49, 52

Baltimore, Chesapeake, and Richmond Steamboat Company 33, 35-36, 41, 43
Baltimore (steamer, 1885) 44
Benjamin B. Odell (steamer, 1911) 56
Boston (steamer, 1924) 105
British Ministry of War Transport 107
Brown, Alexander Crosby 11, 76

Cannon, Captain James 27
Canton Inside Line 87
Carolina (steamer, 1877) 38, 41
Carolyn (icebreaker tugboat) 135
Carville (seagoing tugboat) 145
Chapman, Captain Samuel Boyd 114, 120, 135, 138-141
Charlotte (steamer, 1889) 43, 52
Chesapeake (steamer, 1817) 17
Chesapeake and Potomac Hurricane of 1933 93
Chesapeake Bay Line, Inc. 147-148
Chesapeake Steamship Company 45, 47-49, 51-52, 54-55, 57, 61-62, 65-68, 71, 74-75, 78, 82, 91, 94
City of Annapolis (steamer, 1913) 52, 65-66
City of Atlanta (steamer, 1922) 65-66
City of Baltimore (steamer, 1911) 51-53, 56-57, 66, 71-75
City of Norfolk (steamer, 1911) 8-9, 17, 51-52, 54, 56-57, 65-66, 70, 73, 75, 78, 88-93, 95, 100-101, 103-104, 108, 110-111, 113, 118-121, 124, 127, 129-135, 137, 140-144, 146, 148-149
City of Richmond (steamer, 1913) 52-53, 65-67, 73-75, 82, 95, 100-101, 103, 108, 110-111, 113-114, 118-121, 124, 128-131, 133-147
Clotworthy, Mrs. E. Baker 55-56
Clyde, Thomas 31-32
Colonial Navigation Company 68, 112
Columbia (steamer, 1907) 49, 52-53
Columbus (steamer, 1829) 18- 20
Compton, Key 51, 54, 62
Conifer (icebreaker) 135
Convoy RB-1 105-106

Danville (steamer, 1882) 36-37
District of Columbia (steamer, 1925) 72, 111, 113, 117-118, 122, 124-126, 128, 130-131, 133, 135, 139, 141, 144
Dunn, Robert E. 71, 94, 99, 133-134, 137-138

Eagle (steamer, 1813) 18
Eastern Steamship Company 68
Eaton, Captain Edward H. 122-123
Elisha Lee (steamer, 1892) 113

Eolus (steamer, 1864) 31, 85
Exodus 1947, ex-*President Warfield* (steamer, 1928) 114-117
Epstein, Jacob 61
Falls, Moor N. 29
Ferguson, Benjamin F. 18
Florida (steamer, 1876) 35-36, 39
Florida (steamer, 1907) 47, 49-51, 54, 56, 58, 104-105
Floridian (container freighter, 1960) 137
Foster, R. Sidney 58
Foster, Reuben 33, 41, 43, 45, 51

Gaston (freighter, 1881) 41, 85-87
Georgia (steamer, 1836) 20, 24-26, 30-31
Georgia (steamer, 1887) 36, 38-39, 47
Georgeanna (steamer, 1859) 29, 31
George Leary (steamer, 1864) 31-32
George Peabody (steamer, 1857) 28-29
Gibbs, William Francis 58
Golden Harvest (ocean freighter) 68
Great Eastern (steamship, 1859) 28

Haganah 114
Havana (steamer, 1864) 34
Henderson, Andrew F. 18, 22
Herald (steamer, 1842) 23-25, 31
Hoffberger, Charles 146, 148
Hoffman, Richard Curzon 41-42
Hogshire, Leigh G. 136-137
Hooper, W. Dwight 136
Houseboat cruises 71, 135
Hygeia Hotel 31

Interstate Commerce Commission 94-95

James, Captain Edward 91-92
James T. Brady (steamer) 31
Jamestown Exposition 49, 131
Jewess (steamer, 1838) 20, 24-25

Kentucky (steamer, 1833) 19

Leary Line 31
Lincoln, Mary 30
Louise (steamer, 1864) 39
LSD conversion plan 124, 127

Marine Allied Workers 128-130
Maritime Administration, U.S. 148
Maritime Commission, U.S. 111
Marshall, Captain John L. 66, 91-92
Maryland (steamer, 1907) 113
Maryland and Virginia Steamboat Company 19-20
Maryland Clipper, ex-LST 971 (coastal freighter) 135
Mayo, Captain Wyndham R. 33-34
Medora (steamer, 1842) 22-24
Mellena (AKA transport) 121
Merchants and Miners Transportation Company 112, 118, 129
Meteor (steamer, 1899) 110-111
Morgan, J. Pierpont 41
Mount Vernon (steamer, 1846) 85

Naushon (steamer, 1929)105-106, 108
New Bedford (steamer, 1928) 105-106, 108
New Jersey (freighter, 1862) 32-33, 84
New York (steamer, 1924) 105-106
New Yorker (container freighter, 1960) 137
Norfolk (steamer, 1817) 19
Norfolk, Baltimore, and Carolina Line 136-137
Northland (steamer, 1911) 101, 104-108, 111

Old Bay Line Centennial 80-81, 95- 99
Old Bay Line merger with Chesapeake Line 68, 94, 99
Old Point Comfort 9, 17, 24, 27-32, 37, 47, 49, 62, 66, 83, 92, 113, 117-118, 122, 131-134

Parker, Captain Patrick L. 17, 91-92, 95, 104, 111, 120, 135, 137-138, 140-141
Patrick Henry (steamer, 1832) 19
Peoples' Line 32, 35, 43
Petersburg (steamer, 1856) 19, 85
Philadelphia (steamer, 1860) 28
Philadelphia, Wilmington, and Baltimore Railroad 87
Pocahontas (steamer, 1829) 19-22, 24
Portsmouth and Roanoke Railroad 22
Potomac (steamer, 1894) 66
Powhatan Steamboat Company 24, 28, 33
President Warfield (steamer, 1928) 56, 62-64, 66, 68-69, 71, 80-81, 87, 95, 97-98, 101-104, 106-109, 112-113, 115, 118, 121, 124, 134
Provincetown, ex-*District of Columbia* (steamer, 1924) 72, 141, 143, 146 149

Queen Mary (steamship, 1936) 104

Raleigh (freighter, 1906) 58, 85-86
Richmond (steamer, 1890) 19
Richmond and York River Railroad 33
Roanoke (freighter, 1871) 85
Robinson, John 32
Rogers, Moses 18
Scania (AKA transport, 1944) 121
Scott, Roland 112
Seaboard (freighter, 1874) 85
Seaboard Air Line Railroad 32, 36, 47, 55, 57, 80
Seaboard and Roanoke Railroad 28, 36, 84
Seaboard-Bay Line Company 57
Seafarer's Union 128, 135
Sherwood, John 51
Shirley (freighter, 1874) 35, 85
South Carolina (steamer, 1835) 20
Southern Railway 33, 41, 47, 68, 95
Southland (steamer) 101, 105-108
Spear's Wharf 19-21, 26
Spencer, Samuel 41
State of Maryland (steamer, 1922) 57-61, 66, 71, 75, 78-79, 87, 91-92, 95, 100-102, 108, 121, 124
State of Virginia (steamer, 1923) 57-59, 61-62, 68, 70-72, 87, 95, 100-102, 108, 121, 124, 135
Surprise (steamer, 1817) 19

Tennessee (steamer, 1898) 44-45
Thomas A. Morgan (steamer, 1854) 30, 32, 84
Thomas Kelso (steamer, 1865) 31-32
Transit (freighter, 1864) 32, 84-85
Trippe, Edward 17-18

U-boats (German submarines *U-216, U-96, U-91, U-404, U-619*) 106
Union Dock 26-27, 39, 41, 45-46
Union Line 17
United States Railroad Administration 53-54

Vanoc (British destroyer) 105
Veteran (British destroyer) 105-106
Virginia (steamer, 1817) 18-19
Virginia (steamer, 1879) 36-37, 39, 41
Virginia (steamer, 1905) 42, 44-49, 54
Virginia Clipper, ex-*LST 1145* (coastal freighter) 136-137
Virginia Lee (steamer, 1929) 101, 105

Warfield, S. Davies 54-57, 61
War Shipping Administration, U.S. 100, 110
West Point, Virginia 33-34, 36, 41, 43, 48, 53, 65, 100
Westover (freighter, 1873) 85
William Selden (steamer, 1851) 28-29, 85
Wills, Benjamin B. 141, 143 144, 146
Wood, H. Graham 11

York River Line 33-34, 45, 48, 52, 95, 100
Yorktown (steamer, 1928) 66-67, 75, 95, 101-102, 104-107, 121, 124

About the Author

JACK SHAUM is a retired award-winning print and broadcast journalist who spent nearly fifty years in the business. He is the author of *Lost Chester River Steamboats: From Chestertown to Baltimore*, a history of steam navigation on Maryland's Chester River. He is co-author of *Majesty at Sea*, a history of early twentieth century passenger liners, and co-ghost writer and co-editor of *Night Boat on the Potomac*, the history of the Norfolk and Washington Steamboat Company. He is the former editor-in-chief of the quarterly journal of the Steamship Historical Society of America. He lives near Chestertown, Maryland.

About the Photographer

A native of Baltimore, Maryland, award-winning photojournalist, Hans Marx had a love of steamships. He had a special fondness for the Old Bay Line and never missed an opportunity to photograph and record its historic journey over many years. He bid the line farewell aboard the *City of Norfolk* on her final voyage.